Academic Success Formula

How Ordinary Students Get Extraordinary Results

tutor doctor

How learning hits home.

 FriesenPress

Suite 300 - 990 Fort St
Victoria, BC, V8V 3K2
Canada

www.friesenpress.com

ISBN
978-1-4602-8436-0 (Hardcover)
978-1-4602-8437-7 (Paperback)
978-1-4602-8438-4 (eBook)

1. *EDUCATION*

Distributed to the trade by The Ingram Book Company

Acknowledgements

With over 400 locations in more than a dozen countries, the Tutor Doctor family spans the globe. The people who run these offices, who spend their time helping their communities are more than just business owners — they are thought leaders, working on the front lines with students and families every day. We have helped over 250,000 students and families achieve their goals, and in doing so we've been able to identify the success principles that allow people to succeed not just in academics, but in life. Tutor Doctor would like to thank each and every one of our franchise owners because it is this hard-earned expertise that made a book like this possible. We would especially like to express our gratitude for those franchise owners who were gracious enough to take the time to write the wonderful and informative chapters in this book. Margot Bartsch, Kim Bjarnasson, Gavin Hopper, Chris Lien, Jon-Anthony Lui, Steve Magat, Ashley Mulcahy, Bob Rosedale, and Alex Scotchbrook your hard work is very much appreciated. A special thank you also to Nikki Fotheringham and Melissa Hugel for their efforts in getting this book completed.

Table of Contents

1. Introduction

Worrying about your child has to be one of the most heart-rending feelings in the human experience. When you know something's not right, nothing is right. There's tension at the dinner table, you can't sleep, and you're desperate to find a solution. Whether your child is a straight 'A' student who inexplicably slipped to 'Cs', or you're just praying for a passing grade, you can sense that the problem is really more than academics. Everything is affected, and you just want your kid—and your life—to get back to normal.

In those moments, we all want to crack the code for our child's success. It's no wonder that so many schools, learning centers, software programs, television shows, books, companies, and even politicians all promise to give us a one-size-fits-all prescription to make our education worries go away. They'll plug our kids in and crank out success. It's a tempting idea. Everywhere we turn, whether online, at school, on TV, or even on Craigslist, there's another service offering to make our children happy and successful by "cracking the code" to education.

The reality, though, is there's no single recipe for academic success. Every mechanical approach results in more frustration and more pain for countless parents and students. There are boxes we can't be crammed into, categories that don't work, and equations that don't add up. I was stunned recently when I browsed the site of one well-known educational service provider that recommended a tutor based only on a subject and grade. Surely you need to know more about my child than his age and his class before you can understand how to help him! Is every seventh-grade boy who struggles in algebra the same? As parents, we want a proven, expert approach, but we also understand that there's more to our children than a few academic variables.

The true formula for success is different for every student. It's a unique blend of the parents, teachers, family, mentors, friends, schools, skills, interests, activities, emotions, experiences, and events that shape each student's situation. Only when those factors are understood can a tutor or teacher build an approach to success that meets a student where they are today—physically, mentally, and even emotionally. More often than not, students don't need another diagnosis, survey, or test. Perhaps they just need a listening ear—someone who will take the time to have a conversation and understand their unique needs long before opening a textbook. You can't force a kid to know something. You've got to get to know the kid.

Maybe your student has an off-the-charts IQ but just needs a little help getting organized. Or maybe the problem is a classroom situation that's leaving them behind. Or maybe they just need a little extra time to wrap their head around the assignment. Maybe the problem has nothing to do with the classroom at all but stems from poor nutrition or fitness. Or another, bigger problem in their personal life. Regardless, all those dynamics have to be understood and factored into the formula for academic success that truly meets the student where they are today.

This book is about helping ordinary students get extraordinary results. Tutor Doctor owners, educational consultants, staff, and tutors come from many different walks of life, different educational backgrounds, and diverse perspectives. But they all come together to help students. And most importantly, they come together *where the student is today*: not where they should be according to some model or benchmark.

This book is about real-world stories. You won't see a lot of data, charts, or graphs. That's not because Tutor Doctor's approach doesn't generate real results; 95% of clients recommend us to others. Tutor Doctor professionals tell the stories they do because that's the foundation for their work. When they sit down with a student for their first meeting, they're bringing to the table best practices from hundreds of thousands of personal experiences and relationships.

Right now, you might be frustrated that you can't connect with your child, or that you don't know where to turn. You might feel betrayed by the schools and teachers who aren't giving your daughter the attention she deserves, or that aren't making the effort to understand your son's situation. You might even feel guilty that you haven't been able to make any headway. Or maybe you're just worried—worried that the problem is going to get worse, or that there's something else going on, or that your children won't find the success you want for them.

It is my genuine hope that you find some comfort and useful advice in the stories here. Whatever your situation, know that there's hope. Tutor Doctor has played a role in helping hundreds of thousands of struggling students achieve extraordinary results when they earn that 'B+', when they receive an Ivy League acceptance letter, or even when they become a tutor themselves to help other students excel. Most importantly, this book will get you thinking about your own student's unique situation, and what ingredients might be a part of their distinct formula. Ultimately, knowledge is about so much more than knowing the answer. It's about knowing the student.

Frank Milner, President
Tutor Doctor®

2. Being the Best You Can Be

2.1 Envisioning an 'A' Student: Developing a Growth Mindset

By Alex Scotchbrook

Alex is a Tutor Doctor Education Consultant and Franchise Owner who cares passionately about helping others develop a love of learning. She took the plunge and started her own business following a long and successful career at IBM, where her roles encompassed Operations, Sales, and her biggest passion: Training and Coaching. Having seen the power of 1:1 coaching in adults in her final role at IBM, the transition to an education franchise was an obvious choice for her—Tutor Doctor provided the proven, solid business structure and the high degree of integrity that Alex needed to thrive. Alex was the first person to bring the Tutor Doctor model to the UK in February 2009. Since then, she and her wonderful support team have helped over 1,700 students become confident, happy learners who know how to be the best they can be.

"It is not in the stars to hold our destiny but in ourselves."
—Attributed to William Shakespeare

Almost every parent I meet at a family consultation is very keen to impress upon me that they are not a Pushy Parent or a Tiger Mum. They just know deep down that something could be easier, better, more secure for their child in their learning experience. That is the goal they hold in their gut, which is usually expressed as the more simplified goal of "I feel he can get an A if he tries," or "I don't want her to be moved to the bottom set."

If we merely address the grades of students by imparting knowledge, we miss the true goal, which is to help the student develop their own positive strategies to make the process of learning a safe and enjoyable experience leading to personal fulfillment.

Emma's Story

Meet Emma, a vivacious, open-hearted eight-year-old with a big smile and a great desire to please. Emma was a very popular girl at school but received average effort grades because of her tendency to be quiet in class.

Whilst Emma was happy to chat about the photos around her house, she shut off completely when I asked the simple question, "What do you like doing best at school?" She couldn't figure out what she thought I wanted her to say and gave a huge, theatrical shrug. This pattern of shutting down continued throughout the consultation.

Emma did a math assessment on her own while Mum and I discussed her school reports and areas to focus on for tutoring. In this time, Emma perfectly completed 80 percent of her assessment, with the correct answer neatly written in the box and no workings-out on the page. But there were questions left completely blank throughout the assessment. When I pointed out the first one, Emma did one of her famous big shrugs and smiled coyly at me. So I coached her through the thinking required; she followed the process perfectly and came up with the right result every time, with great celebrations at the end when a drum roll revealed the correct answer! This was a fun process, with Emma completely engaged in the mystery tour of discovering how to work things out. At every step, I was careful to praise Emma for her thinking, her effort, her tenacity. I was equally careful to avoid praise such as "clever girl," "you're good at math," or "you're intelligent."

Why? Because of a growing amount of research that demonstrates the importance of mindset when it comes to effective learning. Carol Dweck, a Stanford psychologist, studied thousands of students to investigate the different effects of mindset on student motivation, tenacity, and grades over time.[1] These thousands of eleven- to twelve-year-old students were divided into two groups: a group of regular students, and a second group who underwent brief training based on the research behind "Growth Mindset." One year after this intervention, the students in the Growth Mindset group were noticeably more engaged and more motivated, especially when challenged, with overall grades on an upward trajectory and significantly higher than those in the first group. The other students were less motivated when challenged and had lower grades on a downward trajectory.

Dweck's study helps us identify two distinct groups of students:

- *Fixed Mindset students* — who believe that you're clever or you're not; there's a "math gene"—some people can do it, some people can't; if you get it wrong, you're just not that clever.

- *Growth Mindset students* — who believe that everybody can learn and that the learning process involves trying out new things and making mistakes along the way.

Dweck's research from MRI scans shows that whenever a student makes a mistake in school, they develop a new synapse. Every time! No brain growth occurs when a student gets all the answers right. Growth Mindset students understand that we are actively growing our brain and our capacity for learning when we make mistakes and that we will get there in the end through perseverance and application.

> *"I'm telling you this because I believe in you."*

Another element of Dweck's study was that, as part of their normal school coursework, students wrote a literary appraisal and received critical feedback on their work. The Growth Mindset students also received one extra line of comment, which said simply, "I'm telling you this because I believe in you." The teachers did not know which of their students received the extra sentence. After one year, the students with this extra comment were performing at a significantly higher level than those who did not have this extra acknowledgment. The expression of belief from a teacher had a powerful and lasting effect on the students, who were reported to have increased their efforts across all subjects as a result of their changed self-image.

Emma, our little eight-year-old, is already thinking like most of us: that she knows or she doesn't, making mistakes means she's not clever, and we're just born like that. Imagine the joy on her face as she worked out something for herself for the first time, something she thought she "just didn't know." You could see her focused interest in that one meeting, and I know that over time, she will develop the habits and love of learning that naturally come when you realize your own brain is changing and growing all the time as you learn to master new things and make mistakes along the way. The natural fear of looking stupid by getting it wrong becomes replaced by a sense of safety in knowing that this is what learning feels like.

> *The student starts to develop a feeling in their gut that they CAN get there and that they're growing all the time.*

Over time, a Growth Mindset student learns to break down a seemingly impossible task into a series of smaller questions. These become mini-challenges to overcome by taking what they know and using it to solve the problem. They learn how to successfully initiate tasks, control their emotions, and focus their attention. The more they practice, the more embedded these methods become as a way of approaching challenges. This, in turn, creates a positive spiral of genuine interest, a desire to learn, a willingness to risk getting it wrong by applying oneself fully, and all the self-esteem and feelings of accomplishment that those things bring. The student starts to develop a feeling in their gut that they *can* get there and that they're growing all the time. It is this gut feeling that encourages the conscious mind to create the conditions for success.

When we help young children like Emma adopt a Growth Mindset, the improved grades go hand-in-hand with security and the confidence that their efforts will get them there, every time.

But what happens when a young student is so afraid of failure that they will do anything to avoid learning?

Toby's Story

Toby was a boy who had lost all sense of his ability to grow. A bright ten-year-old who loved cricket, Toby's blue eyes filled with tears and his face flushed alarmingly when his mum asked him to tell us the time from the big kitchen clock. He couldn't even say the word "math" out loud and had a phobic reaction every time the subject was raised. His genuine fear and distress was heartbreakingly plain to see.

Toby had 'glue-ear' for his first three years of schooling, a condition that rendered him almost deaf in a classroom situation. He had missed out completely on the important basic foundations needed to learn in years four, five, and six. If good learning was as simple as imparting knowledge, Toby would be caught up and ready to go in a matter of weeks. However, it was clear that Toby was a deer in the headlights who couldn't speak, let alone think, when faced with the simplest math task. He had no processing problems and was in every other way a bright, intelligent boy ... so what was going on inside him to produce this phobic response?

A new study by a team of scientists at Stanford University's School of Medicine[2] sheds interesting light on what is happening inside our brains when we experience that "mind gone blank" feeling under stress. Participants were asked to perform a math test under time pressure. MRI scans of their brains revealed that when the "fear" areas of the brain showed increased activity, the problem-solving areas, especially working memory, had decreased activity. In other words, when your brain registers high anxiety, it loses the ability to simultaneously hold several facts in mind, which is essential in order to solve mathematical problems and to concentrate.

One of the therapists at the Priory Group of hospitals, which specialize in mental health, explains this in very simplified terms to help us understand without needing a degree in neuroscience. Imagine your brain is like a giant beach ball. The front of the brain is where the "clever" part is, the part we use to perform complex calculations, to work out nine times seven, or to recall our shopping list from memory. The back half is the "animal" part of the brain that keeps us safe. This tells the rest of our system when we are in danger and puts us into Fight, Flight, or Freeze mode so that we can stay safe from predators. If a tiger walked into the room right now, you would need to fight it with all your strength, run away fast, or freeze so absolutely that it might not notice you. To get your body ready, blood pumps into your muscles and your heart rate increases. Blood flows away from other areas where it isn't needed: you don't need to digest your food when running from a tiger, or to heal the tiny scratch on your hand, or to remember nine times seven. So digestion, the immune system, and logical thinking are all effectively inaccessible when our animal brain tells us we are in danger. The front part of our beach ball brain, the "clever" part, is left high and dry, and our processing is impaired.

The problem for us twenty-first-century beings is that this part of the brain does not understand modern stresses, such as being late in traffic, exam nerves, or fear of failure. It reacts exactly as if we were running away from a tiger, even though our survival is not under any real threat. Thus, the student who gets stressed about their studies is actually cutting off access to the most critical parts of their brain for learning and will feel (and be) a lot less capable than their natural potential dictates as a result of this.

> *A direct, conventional approach to teaching him math will clearly not work until his habitual response is changed.*

Young Toby's brain and body are therefore creating a response to his fear of math to protect him, but at the same time rendering him incapable of taking positive action to fill in his missing foundations by shutting off the very parts of the brain needed to strategize and to learn. A direct, conventional approach to teaching him math will clearly not work until his habitual response is changed, and he learns to feel differently about math and to believe that he, like all people, is capable of growth, change, and learning.

Explaining the workings of the brain and its effect on the body is too cerebral an approach to take with a young child, so we tackled the problem from another angle. The whole family watched me draw out the "building blocks" principle.

Our education is like building a big brick wall. Every year of school is a layer in the wall, and every different idea or concept we learn is a brick in that layer. Most children miss at least one brick each year, through absence or distraction, and this is normal. Unfortunately, with our very large class sizes, teachers do not have time to check what each child has mastered and which bricks need to be re-laid in the wall. The following year, the students start a new layer in the wall, with new bricks that build upon the previous year's foundations. The student may be listening attentively in class, but if they don't have the foundations necessary to understand what they are hearing, they will feel that they "just don't get it." Very quickly, this can encourage a fixed mindset of "I can't do it." And yet the problem is not one of inherent ability but simply of missing foundations.

When Toby's family saw the picture I had built of the cumulative effect of missing foundations, I could see their shoulders coming down and the stress melting away. Even Toby's little face showed that precious thing—hope. He didn't know how, but in that moment he believed that I was going to find someone to help him feel more comfortable and happy at school. The "building blocks" analogy had persuaded him that there was a tiny possibility he wasn't stupid after all. His heart joined us at the table, as well as his head.

His parents and I agreed on a plan. Toby and his tutor didn't do traditional math at all for their first few sessions: no paper and pen, no books, no mention of math! Instead, they played cricket in the garden—something Toby loves and knows he is good at. They covered the foundations of numeracy through play. After a few sessions, the tutor whispered to Toby, "You don't have to tell anyone, but we've been doing math!" They then sat down and looked at all the things he had successfully worked out in the context of school. Toby's chest swelled with pride as he showed his mum everything he had learned. It was one of the happiest phone calls I have received in my years as an Education Consultant, hearing that that young person would now be happy at school and had enough self-belief to stay with the learning process until he truly understood—a far cry from the helplessness he felt at the outset.

Neuropsychologist Rick Hanson and neurologist Richard Mendius write[3] in a very accessible way about the interactions between mind and brain, and use the findings of neuroscience to explain what self-help books have always taught: you can change your mind to change your brain. When you change your brain you change your mind! Thanks to positive role-modelling, enjoyment of the process, and encouragement from his tutor, Toby changed his reflexive, gut instinct that doing math was threatening to his sense of self. As he happily added, subtracted, multiplied, and divided whilst playing cricket, his visceral reaction to math changed—and so did his brain chemistry. Instead of cutting off parts of his brain due to fear, he engaged his whole mind and began a process of literally growing new synapses in his brain.

This knowledge that we can structurally change our brains by changing our minds about something is truly a message of hope that is now scientifically proven. It also underlines the importance of our whole selves showing up to the learning process.

Kate's Story

Seventeen-year-old Kate was a wonderful example of this. She had always been a good student and was aiming for the highest grades in her final school exams. But I got a call from her mum just six weeks before exams started, as Kate was in a state of despair. Earlier in the year, her biology teacher had left for paternity leave with half a unit's syllabus untaught. The class had been merged with another group who had already covered the missing pieces. Kate saw the amount she had to cover as a huge, unapproachable, amorphous THING that she didn't believe she could master, and she had no idea where to start. She had never had any trouble learning, but her belief was that the departure of her teacher meant she was without resources and would fail. She began to talk faster and faster, as her breath became shallow and her brow creased in an anxious frown. Anxiety was taking over.

I asked Kate to think of herself as an 'A' student, who knows deep down that she has everything she needs inside herself to be the best she can be. She sighed deeply, her breathing slowed, her brow smoothed, and she seemed to be picturing this 'A' student as if meeting an old friend. I asked her what 'A' students would do in this situation, how they would define the problem, what first steps they would take, and what resources they would use. I went on to ask her how she would balance her time between biology and her other, equally important subjects. I asked her how much rest time she needed each day to stay at peak performance, whether she felt she could laugh and enjoy herself each day, and which foods she thought would best support her concentration and give her energy. At no point did I "tell" her anything.

Kate's own sense of her innate potential to be a high-performing student led her to realize that she had everything inside her needed to master the problem without burning out or sacrificing other subjects. She also realized that a tutor would help fill in the missing elements of the syllabus—an outside resource that would give her confidence that she was on track. She almost perfectly described that wonderful state of flow a student has when they know what they have to do and when they are going to do it. The body collaborates with the mind to achieve a goal when it has been primed by thought on how to achieve it easily and naturally, whilst enjoying the effort leading to results as a natural state of achievement.

> *Constantly trying to use your efforts to change the outer world is what leads to burnout.*

Kate established a real sense of the path to her goal. Having broken down the conditions that would lead her there, she could see success in her mind. As Richard Mendius says, "It's the inner skills that make the greatest difference." Kate could have followed her knee-jerk instinct to try to change the outer world by wishing her teacher had not left or by sweating over her textbooks day and night to try to master new, advanced learning alone. Constantly trying to use your efforts to change the outer world is what leads to burnout. It can't usually be done, so we multiply our efforts and keep trying, eventually running out of steam and hope. But by reconnecting her with her inner world, I was able to engage Kate's whole sense of self.

I changed her reaction to the outer world by connecting her to her sense of personal power and efficacy.

Max's Story

One of the most important jobs I have at a family consultation is to make sure that the student is fully committed to the process of learning—mind and body. If they are not, it's like pouring water into a vessel with the lid still on. Fifteen-year-old Max admitted that his English could use some help, as he needed to pass to get into technical college for his final two years of school. As with Kate, I asked him to imagine he was an 'A' student, but Max very quickly interrupted and told me he didn't want to be an 'A' student because 'A' students have no friends and work all the time!

His inner memory, or unconscious mind, believed it had evidence that excelling academically would mean having no life. This was not a belief Max had previously been aware of, but it was clear that he would not align himself fully with a goal of success if his inner thoughts were telling him he would lose out. His unconscious mind and conscious mind were not working together, which creates friction and tension, with a lot of energy spent as the brain figures out which way to go.

Our brain is a complex network of neural connections, with "go/don't go" switches that determine which areas to use for any given situation. Of our myriad beliefs about who we are in the world and what makes us safe, the most embedded ones win. Max "knew" that he had to pass his English exam, but his more powerful belief was that to excel meant losing status, friendship, and freedom. We needed to find him a goal that was true to him so that he didn't sabotage his endeavors by creating mental blocks. Through further coaching, he found that he did want to be able to use words better to be funny, articulate, and efficient in all his exams. This removal of the conflict between his aspirations meant his brain was now set to "work with itself."

Neurobiologist Carla Schatz tells us that when neurons are firing together, they get wired together too.[4]

When we start to think in a certain way, it's like a trickle of water on a slope. Over time, the trickle creates a well-worn groove, and the passage of water becomes quicker and easier, eventually forming a powerful stream. The more familiar something becomes, the more likely we are to do it. The more we do it, the easier it gets. Scientists can tell whether they are looking at an MRI scan of a pianist's brain or a taxi driver's brain by seeing where cells have thickened and multiplied through use in the areas of fine motor function or visual-spatial memory.

There's more news about our brains that we can use to great advantage: the brain does not distinguish between an actual experience and a vividly imagined one. If you have ever woken up from a nightmare in a cold sweat with your heart pounding, you have experienced this first-hand, albeit in a negative way. Fortunately, we can also use our thoughts deliberately to turn far-off goals into long-lost friends inside our minds.

This is why sports coaches encourage mental rehearsal, in which, for example, footballers imagine scoring goals over and over again. When felt vividly—when you hear the crowds, feel the grass underfoot, and see the ball flying into the goal—this prepares you for success just as much as hours of physical practice. Researchers at Ohio University conducted an experiment: for four weeks, a group visualized themselves exercising for 11 minutes per day, five days per week.[5] A second group did not. At the end of the four weeks, the group that had visualized themselves exercising was TWICE as strong as the group that hadn't! The brain takes instructions from our thoughts every bit as much as it does from our actions, so we can improve our performance by visualizing ourselves being successful and believing it.

For Max, this meant he could perform far better with the same amount of effort, leaving time to spare for fun and laughter with friends. Only his focus needed to change.

Our Whole Self Needs to Show Up to the Learning Process

Emma, Toby, Kate, and Max all show us how our whole self needs to show up to the learning process. Emma's fixed mindset stopped her from seeing that through effort, challenges could become interesting and engaging. Toby's fear blocked the very parts of his brain that he needed to perform, and until he was able to think differently, learning was impossible. Kate was a victim of circumstance, and stress stopped her seeing herself as an achiever, while Max just couldn't see any joy in doing his best.

By asking the right questions, we can change the way a student perceives that 'A' grade—or any form of outstanding success. You're not a pushy parent for wanting the best for your child! Helping them to see success as part of their whole life is the difference between an experience that is painful and difficult and one that is enjoyable and pleasurably stretching. Because our physical bodies respond to the thoughts in our mind, we must see beyond the need to "know our stuff." Our brains are designed to grow and learn, so we can believe that success is already inside us, just waiting to come out.

"A man is but the product of his thoughts.
What he thinks, he becomes."
—Mahatma Gandhi

2.2 Thinking with the End in Mind—Keep Goals in Sight

By Ashley Mulcahy

Ashley Mulcahy is a San Diego State University alumna, and she is our youngest franchisee to date. After receiving her bachelor's degree, Mulcahy bought the Tutor Doctor franchise for which she'd been working, and now, at twenty-six, she heads an education empire that contracts with more than 100 tutors in more than 20 cities. She is a native Floridian and resides in Orange County, California, with her husband, Ray, and their dog, Kirby.

Author Stephen Covey believes that all things are created twice. We first construct things in our mind, and it is then that they can come into physical being. This is one of my favorite concepts because it applies to so many aspects of life. Covey introduces the idea in his bestselling classic, *The 7 Habits of Highly Effective People.*[6] Once we accept the truth of the quote, we can then further interpret the "begin with the end in mind" theory Covey presents. He says that we should start with an image or picture in our heads of the end of our lives, and use this as a frame of reference. What he means is, by imagining how our life will end up, we can be the architect developing the blueprint for our life.

We often live in our fast, day-to-day lives and we think that things happen TO us. When you break it down and look at it more closely, you realize there was a planned thought that had to occur in order for that particular outcome to take place. This type of thinking was made popular in the bestseller *The Secret*, but how does it actually apply to your real-life situation? We often see people who seem to have it better than we do. A kid who gets an 'A' on an exam that your child had to study twice as long for, who gets into your child's dream school and considers it their "back up", who gets a great job fresh out of college, maybe even without a student loan to pay off thanks to a scholarship. People are so quick to think that these others just have it easier and must have more "luck."

Truth is, we don't ever sit down and really think about what it took for them to achieve their goals. We don't hear about their struggles and all the behind-the-scenes work it took for them to succeed. We don't see the late nights studying or the time spent interning before that great job was offered. In this day and age, we see someone post on Facebook that they graduated as valedictorian, and we think, "Why can't my child be like that?" However, that same person isn't going to be posting about the trials and tribulations involved in achieving their goal.

We must first come to the understanding that we create our own future. Every action is a result of a choice that you had to think about. As an Education Consultant, one of my first questions to a student is, "What are you hoping to achieve?" They often look at me and say, "Good grades."

"Ok yes, but what about after that? So you get good grades, then what?" This conversation, right away, helps me to understand how goal-driven the student is. Yes, you might aim to get an 'A' in an exam or go to university, but what is that working toward? Then they might say something along the lines of "I want to be a doctor." From here, we work backwards to see how they can reach that goal. I want all of my students to start with the end result and then work backwards. I get a lot of crazy looks from students, especially the ones who say, "I don't know, I haven't thought about it yet." Is that student going to change their mind a million times before that? Most likely—up to 75 percent of college students change their major at least once.[7] But—the important part is that the student has an end vision they are working towards.

Why Does This Matter?

We live in a culture where people have an "I need it now" mentality—which formally is called instant gratification. "Instant gratification is the desire to experience pleasure or fulfillment without delay or defer-ment. Basically, it's when you want it; and you want it now."[8] You can order coffee with an app now. Show up and it's ready for you. I know this all too well because I come from this generation where everything is accessible at the touch of a button. We get annoyed when our phones are taking a couple of seconds to open a web page. Everything is becom-ing marketed to us so that we can get it as soon as the desire strikes us. A "spend now, save later" mindset correlates to the housing market col-lapse of 2008, and why a lot of my friends already had severe credit card debt in their twenties. Why is this a problem with academics? Well, I see it first-hand with my students. They look at the here and now, which is normal for this age group. Academic success isn't as instantaneous as requesting an Uber driver. It takes a lot of long-term, self-improvement to become a successful student. Note—if you want to be an actor or join the army—the same rules apply.

Struggling Students

I hear a lot of students at consultations who say, "I hate school". This is the number one indicator that the student has no vision of their end goal. Everyone has things in life they don't want to do. I certainly didn't enjoy the late nights studying or working at a restaurant job to pay for my SAT/ACT exams. What made me and others push through this? It's the visual reminder of what I am working towards. When a student does not have their goals in sight, they go back to instant gratification. When given the option to hang out with friends or study for a test, a struggling student immediately chooses their friends. They only see the here and now, not the ramifications of not studying and how this can affect their future.

According to Oprah's popular book club feature *The Secret,* your entire life experience is being formed through the law of attraction, and this is done through your thoughts. When you visualize, you are putting powerful energy into the universe.[9] Whether you believe that or not, keeping sight of your goals works. Famous Olympians use visualization and imagery to improve their performance. When preparing for the Winter Olympics in Sochi, Russia, Olympic skiers went through visualization and imagery techniques to envisage the win. One Alpine skier even said he had the track in his mind throughout the year. He would be in the middle of his normal routine—brushing teeth or showering—while picturing the movements he would make around each corner of the track.[10]

A study surrounding brain patterns in weightlifters found that the patterns triggered when a weightlifter actually lifted hundreds of pounds were also triggered when they only imagined lifting. This shows the true power of our brain. We can truly do anything we set our mind to. If athletes can use visualization to accomplish performance goals, how can we enhance this for students?

Start With a Vision

One of the best ways to start the goal-setting process is to discover what your personal purpose is. In order to help your child, student, or mentee do this you'll need to know what your own purpose is. Start by asking yourself what you want in life. If you don't know what you want, you don't know what you need to achieve to get there. This is actually the fun part. You get to daydream. What do you really want to create for yourself? What does your ideal life look like?

It is never too young to start. I remember when I was in seventh grade, it was the first time I had ever heard of a "vision board". Our project assignment was to cut out pictures from magazines about what our future will look like. A vision board is supposed to be a visual representation of your goals including but not limited to relationships, finance, career, travel, home, and anything else relating to your personal growth. I remember explicitly, my first vision board included a Lexus convertible, a house on the beach, and a job as a lawyer. I had seen too many episodes of *Law & Order: SVU* where becoming an attorney was my dream—starting at thirteen-years-old.

Did I actually become an attorney? No. However, it gave me purpose, even at a young age. I knew I wanted to help others and that it may require a lot of schooling. It made me start thinking about how I would get to those points in my life. The only law school I knew of in seventh grade was Harvard Law—so the image went up on my vision board. I kept the board in a location I could easily look at. When I entered high school, I knew one thing was for sure: I was going to be in school a long time if I wanted to become a lawyer, so I should try to start earning credits now. I was dual-enrolled in college credits. By the time I entered university, I had completed so many university credits that I was already considered an upperclassman. I attribute this to the visual, constant reminder of my end goals.

In the midst of my finance law class at San Diego State, I had to go back to the drawing board and revisit my purpose. This is normal. We change as we grow up, so it is common for our goals to change as we enter new stages in life. Make a point to revisit your vision board, ensuring there is blank space so you can add or alter along the way.

Committing by Writing

Another important step is physically writing down concrete goals. We commit to that goal when we write it down. We often hear goal-setting as a strategy for success, but most people don't even have a measurable and defined goal written down. Mark H. McCormack wrote the bestselling *What They Don't Teach You At Harvard Business School,* which was first published in 1984. In it, he wrote about a fictionalized study done on the 1979 Harvard MBA graduate students who were asked, "Have you set clear, written goals for your future and made plans to accomplish them?" Only 3 percent had written goals and plans, 13 percent had goals but they weren't in writing and 84 percent had no clear goals at all.[11]

Ten years later, the same group was interviewed again and the result was astonishing. In McCormack's fictional scenario, the 13 percent of the class who had goals, but did not write them down was earning twice the amount of the 84 percent who had no goals. The 3 percent who had written goals were earning, on average, 10 times as much as the other 97 percent of the class combined! While McCormack's "study" only looked at earnings to quantify success, I still find it to be an extremely motivating example of why creating clear and measurable goals and writing them down is a key to success.

Closing the Gap

A study from the University of Toronto found that people were able to close the gender and ethnicity gap simply by goal-setting. In the study, a full cohort of undergraduate management students participated in a goal-setting program, where their life goals were formulated and documented. Professors were astounded to see such gaps close to 98 percent.[12] They attributed the success of the goal-setting program to being an intervening force on the students. Students who were not previously motivated started to perform better on exams. The study correlated the increased exam scores to improved self-regulation. Previous studies have shown that self-regulation appears to enhance when specific goals are set,[13] especially when people contrast a fantasized ideal future with present reality.[14] This highlights the importance of detailed, written goals and their power on shifting student performance. We can visualize the goals from our vision board, but if we do not write them down, then there is no commitment. The process of writing these goals down helps to turn your vision of an ideal future into a reality.

As a result, students might attain an internal awareness of their goals and ideal future. In doing so, they will be able to self-regulate and direct energy towards their goals in a more efficient and effective way.[15]

Goals improve self-regulation through their effects on motivation, learning, self-efficacy, and self-evaluations of progress.[16] Initially, people must make a commitment to attain a goal. It won't improve performance without this commitment.[17] Goals motivate people to put in the necessary effort to meet task demands and persist over time. Goals also work to direct attention to the task features most relevant to them, the behaviors they need to perform, and the potential outcomes. Goals can even affect how people process information by helping people focus on the task, select and apply appropriate strategies, and monitor progress.

Self-regulation is very important to people of all ages, students, and non-students. This process allows us to periodically verify if we are sticking with our plan. You wouldn't drive from San Diego to New York City without a map to ensure you're on the right route. Someone who doesn't self-regulate might end up in the wrong location, not having verified where they were at different checkpoints. The same goes for life—how can one live a life without written, defined goals? It's like trying to use a map by relying solely on memory.

As people work on a task, they compare their current performance with the goal. Evaluating our progress strengthens self-efficacy and sustains our motivation. People become busy in their day-to-day world, so it is easy to get off your plan. It is possible to be busy, without being effective.[18] Activity does not equal achievement. A perceived difference between present performance and the goal may lead to dissatisfaction, which can actually enhance effort. Although dissatisfaction may result in quitting, this won't happen if people believe they can achieve success by making a change such as changing their strategy or asking for help. When we achieve our goals, we become more effective people and this leads us to select new, challenging goals.

Despite these benefits, just setting any goals does not automatically enhance self-regulation. Rather, the goal needs to address specificity, proximity, and difficulty to be effective.

How to Set Goals Effectively

Specificity

Goals that incorporate specific performance standards are more likely to improve self-regulation and activate self-evaluations when compared to general goals like "to do my best" or "try hard."[19] Specific goals increase performance because they state the amount of effort required for success and boost self-efficacy by providing a clear standard against which we can measure our progress.

Proximity

Goals are distinguished by how far they project into the future. Proximal, short-term goals are achieved more quickly and result in higher motivation and better self-regulation than more distant, long-term goals.

At the same time, some research shows that proximal goals don't promote performance better than distant goals.[20] One suggestion is that people working toward distant goals should subdivide them into smaller, more manageable tasks, which produces the benefits. Proximal goals strengthen our belief in our ability to achieve our goals because they allow clear and frequent self-evaluations of progress. It's often difficult to determine progress towards a distant goal, so we don't see the same benefits.[21]

Difficulty

Unlike specificity and proximity, goal difficulty does not directly affect performance. Overly easy goals do not motivate; neither are people motivated to attempt what they believe are impossible goals.[22] Assuming that people have the necessary skills, goals that are moderately difficult seem to have the best effects on motivation and self-regulated performance.[23]

Goal setting is an integral component of self-regulation. Setting goals is a strategy that can be applied to so many aspects of our lives. Effective goal setting requires that people set a long-term goal, break it into short-term, attainable sub-goals, monitor progress and assess capabilities, adjust the strategy and goal as needed, and set a new goal when that one is achieved. This plan is the key to promoting improved function, higher motivation and perceived self-efficacy, and self-regulated learning and performance.

Personal Mission Statement

A great way to tie your visualizations and defined goals together is to create a personal mission statement.[24] This is very effective because it helps you to reflect on your character and contributions, rooting into your inner principles and core values. A personal mission statement should be the basis for making life-directing choices and daily decisions.

Reward Yourself

Rewards are an effective motivator. Do you remember as a little kid being told that if you tidied your room you could watch one more episode of your favorite TV show? There is actually merit to dangling the proverbial carrot when facing a tedious task if it helps motivate you to complete it.

Deciding ahead of time to reward yourself once you achieve something can help keep you on the path to success. It can also help keep you clear-minded and consistent. One way to do this is to provide yourself small incentives on the path to a bigger goal. If the end goal is to get an 'A' on a math test, you could reward yourself for each study session, or each homework assignment completed.

Setting goals is obviously significant, but rewarding yourself is almost equally as important. By giving ourselves something to look forward to, we can be motivated to do almost anything.

> *It's never too young to start.*

Goal setting is important in all aspects of our lives because it makes us an active participant in our own future. We can take control of what happens to us by setting out to achieve something, rather than waiting for good things to fall in our lap. The important fact to remember is that it's never too young to start. The earlier we start setting goals for our future, the earlier we can get on the path to success.

2.3 Whose Expectations Matter Most?

By Chris Lien

Chris Lien has developed an international view of education through his twenty-five years in the electronics industry. He earned a B.S. in Electrical Engineering and an MBA with emphasis in Management and Marketing, so he's no stranger to education. During his prior career, he managed engineering, sales, and marketing teams around the world, and obtained insights regarding international best practices in education. He applies these insights to students in San Diego County as their tutors provide academic coaching on a daily basis.

Motivation. Old "Mo". The "Big Mo". A commonly asked question in today's pop culture is "Do you have it in you?" This question pertains to motivation as a driving force rather than God-given abilities. Another saying is "You know it when you see it", indicating the fruits of motivation are evident through action, and that you don't see motivation itself. Much like the wind, we only see its effects.

Athletes, coaches, musicians, pop culture icons, and many other noteworthy figures often tout motivation as the main driver for their success, and their followers want to achieve similar success. What often separates successful from unsuccessful people is not talent or money or other tangible factors, but rather the intangible element of personal motivation. Personal achievement despite adversities is a very common theme of life amongst successful people, indicating that they developed their own strong personal motivation throughout life.

Modern society places great value on the word 'motivation.' An entire industry of public speakers, personal coaches, authors, and training seminars has emerged to help people develop it, both internally and externally. People spend billions of dollars annually to stoke personal motivation in their quest to achieve more in life.

For example, a soccer player who excels relative to their peers and practices daily is often thought to be highly motivated. Meanwhile, someone not as skilled but who wants to improve, and practices daily may not be perceived as highly motivated. Is motivation evident only by results or is there an invisible aspect that eventually becomes evident?

Any discussion on personal motivation must first begin with what it is and is not. Webster's Dictionary defines motivation as:

> *The mental process that arouses an organism to action; as, a large part of a teacher's job is to give students the motivation to learn on their own.*

Or, *the goal or mental image of a goal that creates a motivation*.

Note the first definition involves an external factor whereas the second refers to an internal factor.

Many people have mistakenly assumed that motivation is an end rather than a means to an end. It can best be considered a force that compels a person to take action toward a desired purpose or goal. As seen from these definitions, motivating factors can be both internal and external, and the two types must work in a complementary way for a person's objectives to be attained. This is especially true when a significant investment of time, resources, sacrifice, and effort are required.

Some people claim a person cannot be externally motivated to do something—rather one person can only help another find their inner motivation, which will spur them to achieve their goal. While this might seem like yet another "chicken and egg" scenario, it's true that external motivators can help develop internal motivation for people of all ages. However, internal motivation increases solely based on the (internal) decision of that particular individual.

Getting and staying motivated requires motivation.

Far from a play on words or circular reasoning, this is the key to the battle.

Drawing Analogies from Sports and Other Areas

Many people have a more intuitive understanding of motivation as it relates to sports, the arts, and other areas of personal expression, rather than education. Sports and arts often involve a greater personal investment of energy, emotion, self-expression, and offer a wider range of outcomes than the daily academic routine. These activities are also seen as a relief from "boring" activities like school and work. They can also require much financial investment, especially if a student attends a "free" public school. Yet, students and parents would do well to understand and apply the lessons learned by coaches and other instructors in these areas to their academic lives.

Coaches often strive to model the behaviors they want their athletes to follow. When combined with personal and team goals, this helps to increase individual motivation to meet one's own goals. They often try to motivate their athletes to maintain perseverance as a way to remove impulsiveness, which would undermine individual or team goals. The objective is to teach a steadiness and discipline that will help the athlete go on to greater achievements, regardless of circumstances, temporary performance levels, or whether anyone is monitoring their actions.

Coaches point to several key factors that combine to form motivation in superior athletes, many of which are unrelated to the skills or gifts an athlete is born with. These include:

- Goal-orientation

- Teachability

- Perseverance

- Self-control

- Accountability

- Others-orientation

- Tireless work ethic

These traits can't be acquired simply by reading about them, they can't be purchased, and they are not maintained except by continuous application over the course of one's life. The same holds true for students at any age, especially high school students finishing their secondary education and starting college preparation. These traits both stem from and lead toward motivation, and without an inner drive to sustain and increase them, motivation will decrease and progress will stall.

> *Genius is one percent inspiration and ninety-nine percent perspiration.* — *Thomas Edison*

Many coaches have said they would rather have a team of average talented individuals with high motivation and teachability, than a team comprised of highly-skilled athletes with low motivation and teachability. Most people can be taught the skills and techniques to excel, but a bad attitude can take an entire lifetime to change, if at all.

Famous inventor Thomas Alva Edison spoke a lot about success, perseverance, and motivation. Two of his most memorable statements are, "Genius is one percent inspiration and ninety-nine percent perspiration", and "Many of life's failures are people who did not realize how close they were to success when they gave up." Edison was familiar with both failure and success, having made hundreds of unsuccessful attempts prior to every triumph, including many of the electrical devices we take for granted today. Without the quiet resolve and strength to not veer from his vision, you might be reading this book on parchment rather than high-quality bound paper or on a screen. Edison quipped near the end of his career, "I haven't failed, I've just found 10,000 ways that won't work", showing he didn't lose motivation or quit when he knew he was having trouble on his path, but instead made course corrections to progress in the right direction.

Many centuries ago, Aristotle related actions, habit, and motivation in the following statement, "We are what we repeatedly do. Excellence, then, is not an act, but a habit." Even in his day, motivation was understood to be the combination of inner and external compunctions to press on in the direction one envisions. Hence, both excellence and slothfulness are purposed—people must determine which trait or end result they want and create plans and support systems to achieve it.

Popular Historical Theories and Perspectives on Human Motivation

Social scientists, psychologists, organizational behaviorists, and corporations for many decades have studied various motivators and their impact on human behavior, for both individuals and organizations.

Abraham Maslow's Hierarchy of Needs[25] was an early study in organizational behavior, which determined five classes of human needs, ranging from physiological drives to a higher-order need for actualization or growth. Many of his contemporaries used this as a framework for analyzing human behavior. Self-actualization was determined as the highest-level thought process one could achieve, and it could be attained only if the lower primary needs and wants were met.

Herzberg[26] devised a simpler two-category model of motives, defined as satisfiers (extrinsic) and motivators (intrinsic). Intrinsic motives were considered as higher-order, and people vary in how they pursue and achieve both types of motives. A person could operate more according to intrinsic motives as a critical mass if their extrinsic motives were satisfactorily met.

In recent decades, goal-setting theory has become a major force in the field of motivation and education. This approach has been widely used in the workplace as performance goals and metrics by students as they form daily, monthly, and term goals and activity plans, and by individuals as they set personal goals. Motivators in achieving these goals are both internal and external, with the external factors tied to rewards including increased pay, higher grades, and other tangible results (e.g. weight loss).

An important modern concept regarding motivation, especially in the education field, is self-efficacy. It is defined as an individual's confidence in his ability to achieve a specific action or succeed in a scenario presented to him. How assertively or decisively one approaches his goals or challenges is highly correlated to his sense of self-efficacy.

Self-efficacy theory[27] has often been coupled with goal-setting theory to help people develop the motivation to achieve their goals, as a person's belief in his/her ability to succeed in specific situations is a major factor in personal motivation. Bandura and other proponents assert self-efficacy reflects confidence in a person's ability to exert control over one's own motivation, behavior, and social environment. Bandura[28] also writes that self-efficacy beliefs influence how people feel, think, motivate themselves, and behave via four major processes—cognitive, motivational, affective, and selection.[29] As a person (young or old) has an experience, these four processes together form the person's perception of the outcome of that experience. Based on the person's perception and involvement, a belief regarding their capability is formed, and they arrive at a summary sense of their own ability to achieve their goals in that scenario.

Self-efficacy consists of four major drivers: mastery experiences, social modeling, social persuasion, and physiological responses. These are a combination of internal and external factors that result in a person assessing their own capability in an experience, and motivation to pursue the experience again in the future. Mastery experiences are a person's prior successes in similar types of activities. Social modeling involves the person having seen someone successfully execute a similar task and that behavior is imitated. Social persuasion involves encouragement or discouragement from another person. It has been found that discouragement has more effect on self-efficacy than does encouragement. A person's physiological responses to stress also affect self-efficacy. A person having low self-efficacy who gets nervous at the thought of a task could conclude it's due to inability, whereas a high self-efficacy person could conclude nervousness is just par for the course regardless of ability.

Taken together, these four drivers can develop a blend of positive and negative feelings and perceptions that form a person's net belief about something. Development of self-efficacy is a lifelong process as people continuously acquire new skills, experiences, and knowledge. As a result, self-efficacy and motivation (both internal and external) impact each other as a person sets out to accomplish a task.

In the case that a person becomes overly confident in their ability to accomplish a specific task or goal, self-efficacy includes a self-regulating feedback element that comes out of trial and error. A negative outcome from an activity can result in a person concluding their ability in that activity is woefully lacking. Depending on whether that activity is beneficial, the person may or may not be encouraged to try it again, or decide to improve the ability to succeed in that endeavor.

Research Studies Prove Motivation Leads to Increased Student Success and Enjoyment

Dozens of other academic and corporate research studies through the decades show internal motivators yield stronger and longer-lasting positive outcomes than external motivators, though the best results happen when both types work together. Bandura and Schunk in 1981[30] studied 40 math students age seven to ten years old. They found self-motivation through proximal goal setting is a very practical means to increase competence, self-efficacy toward the subject, and an increased interest in math (previously, students lacked both the skills and enjoyment). On the other hand, distal goals provided no discernible effects on student achievement or motivation.

A 1996 study[31] by Bandura determined a parent's sense of academic efficacy for their child impacts their academic achievement in a positive way. Children will hold higher beliefs regarding their academic abilities if their parents hold high aspirations for and expectations of them. A child will develop increased self-efficacy, which drives increased academic achievement. Higher levels of student self-esteem and reduced anxiety and depression were also noted as a result. Therefore, self-efficacy is a major component of personal motivation and is especially relevant in education.

Interestingly, gender differences in self-efficacy have been found to result in disproportionate numbers of workers in different fields, most notably fewer women in the STEM (science, technology, engineering, and mathematics) occupations. Many programs have been launched to increase female participation in STEM, with some success so far. However, gender-based gaps in self-efficacy may take time to be reduced completely, as a complex combination of social normative, societal, modeling, peer, and even pop culture factors continue to reinforce stereotypes for girls and young women, leading to their reduced motivation to pursue these fields.

Bringing Motivation Home for Students and Parents

For today's students to be successful, they must possess steely resolve and determination (i.e. motivation), which can be maintained only by moving toward a vision they personally own. Parents, teachers, family, friends, peers, teammates, clergy, and many others can help a student define, refine, and maintain the course toward their goal. In the absence of any of these people in a student's life, encouragement, counsel, and even correction can come from others within the student's group of contacts.

This is why it is important for a student to choose their influencers and counselors wisely, to ensure the external motivation and advice received is constructive and healthy. People with the greatest degree of positive motivation are those who invite people into their lives who offer genuine praise and correction, encouragement, and instruction, and who will lovingly ask the "tough questions," which force a person to revisit their goal and methods of achieving it.

Every person who has achieved great personal success has attributed much of it to the influential people in their life. Academy Award winners' speeches often contain the names of a dozen or more people they believe provided motivation during times when the winner had maybe wanted to quit, or not pursue the project for which the award was given.

Therefore, educators and parents have to encourage students to press on toward growth in their education and other pursuits, to ensure a negative experience in an otherwise worthwhile or necessary endeavor does not crush their motivation. External encouragement and motivation are crucial because they push students to learn, adapt, and grow in their own motivation to explore new ideas and pursuits, especially in areas that require them to go beyond their current skills or comfort zone.

Recommended Ways to Initiate and Increase Student Motivation

Students need to struggle a little in their studies in order to build increased motivation.

Drawing from the experiences of educators, coaches, and others involved in student instruction, I've learned that students need to struggle a little in their studies in order to build increased motivation gained through perseverance. This might seem counterintuitive to the parent of a child who repeatedly asks for help, but this type of "tough love" is vital to form a child's ability to work independently and gain the critical skill of self-discovery. Younger children will tend to be less autonomous than older children, so their needs will need more direct support. Some whining or complaining might be expected when a child is first directed to work more independently, but this is simply human nature. However, if a child expresses strong anxiety or shuts down, parents should work to help them in eventually becoming more independent through smaller initial steps. This will make the task seem less daunting. With all children, praise is crucial as they learn and achieve each correct answer.

Recommendations to Build a Student's Motivation (Internal and External) for Learning

- Wean him/her off total dependence on the parent to accomplish simple tasks and assignments.

- Set age and skill level appropriate goals according to the SMART paradigm (Specific, Measurable, Attainable, Realistic, Time-bound). Start small and progressively increase task complexity and decrease time as appropriate.

- Set and communicate a block of time for independent work and set aside time to answer questions or review the finished product. Intermediate and final checkpoints can be time or event based as best fits the child's age and the type of task to accomplish.

- Evaluate the child's work quantity and quality, and time to completion. It is essential for children to provide an honest self-assessment of the outcome and effort applied. This can become uncomfortable or stressful for them so an environment of acceptance and openness is crucial even if the child gets upset.

Remember! The goal for your child is to develop internal motivation. A negative experience with parent or teacher can prevent them from achieving this.

- Praise the child for the work accomplished, even if it wasn't fully completed or on time. There will be plenty of time to improve work quality and timeliness in the future, and this should start as a positive growth experience. For older kids, in as positive a manner as possible, set the expectation that the next task can be achieved better and faster, to help instill a desire for continuous improvement.

- Reward systems must be implemented to encourage the student to complete each task, and a larger, highly desirable reward should be communicated, to be earned upon completion of the longer-term set of goals. Some children are motivated by external "fun" factors (toys, trinkets, ballgame tickets, desserts, money, etc.) whereas other children are motivated more by internal factors (spoken praise, hugs, pat on the back, awards, recognition, etc.). Many parents find a child will be motivated by a combination of these things.

- Lavish praise is one of the most powerful motivating factors because it includes external acknowledgment by hearers and it builds the child's self-esteem in the process.

- A trial-and-error set of healthy and appropriate ways of stimulating a child's internal motivation should be attempted. Keep a log detailing what works best for each situation.

- Older students or those stuck in a performance plateau can benefit from academic "cross-training" much like performance athletes do. Sometimes changing the order of tasks, location or environment of study, or simultaneous addition and removal of tasks can bring freshness to a student's perspective, and spur him on to rise above a plateau.

Another key recommendation is to ensure your child's teacher recognizes their unique strengths and differences compared to their classmates and teaches at the level best suited for that child. If you feel like this isn't happening, ask the teacher for additional customized instruction or guidance. Also, engaging a tutor or academic coach can be a very powerful and cost-effective means to ensure your child learns all they can, and be better prepared to apply knowledge at the next level of learning.

Conclusion

Each parent must become an excellent student of his or her student(s) to ensure maximized potential and the student's enjoyment of the process.

Life is a journey—education is a journey along life's journey.

Getting and staying motivated requires motivation.

3. The Power of Learning

3.1 The Power of One-to-One Tutoring

By Margot Bartsch

Margot is a business development professional with experience in the development of sales, company branding, marketing, systems, programs and education/training. Previously, she has had the pleasure of taking two companies successfully through transition periods to become leaders in their industry. To accomplish this, she streamlined systems and materials and standardized where appropriate, worked with staff for understanding and buy-in, rebranded marketing materials, and created training materials and strategies for professional development and upgrades of current and new staff. More recently, Margot Bartsch has owned and launched the Tutor Doctor–Fraser Valley franchise with her husband Doug.

While most programs and curricula that students are enrolled in have very specific educational requirements and outcomes, the students in these programs are all unique individuals with their own goals, challenges, needs, personalities, and learning styles. It is often difficult for individual students to "fit into the box" of the system they are a part of. One-to-one tutoring offers the opportunity to help students through these challenges and complete their goals successfully.

I have been working in the Fraser Valley of British Columbia since 2009, helping students reach their potential. We have tutored students ranging in age from three years old to seniors. Some of our students are years behind in school and are working to catch up, while others are desperate to pass an exam so that they can get into a program. WorkSafeBC clients are retraining for a new opportunity and some of our students with disabilities need a tutor to help them get through their academic curriculum. There are also many students working to get scholarships and want straight As!

There's a lot on the line for many of these students, so it's vital that we help them reach their goals, whatever they may be. One-to-one tutoring is the key that gets them there. You can personalize the tutor, the support materials, the goals, and the teaching approach to fulfill the student's unique needs. Watching students get the help they need, and often turning their life and future around, has been one of my greatest joys over the years. One-to-one tutoring is so powerful at helping students reach their potential and achieve their goals.

Mentoring is Key

> Mentoring is not always about school work. It is also developing a relationship with a student to help them gain confidence so they can succeed. One student I was tutoring was initially closed off and hesitant to work with me to the point of being resistant and negative. Over time, she got more comfortable, had her homework done when I arrived and had questions ready. She went from giving up on school and wanting out, to taking on more difficult classes and being engaged, motivated and even driven to get things done. Mentoring her and seeing this transformation was an encouragement to not only her but me as well.
>
> —Meagan, Tutor

I think one of the most underrated facets of tutoring is the mentoring aspect. I find this to be particularly true for students in Grades 4–9. Many young people can really benefit from a good role model and from someone investing in their lives. Finding a tutor that students can look up to is often the catalyst to their success. Every student deserves a tutor who can inspire, motivate, encourage, and make tutoring and learning fun.

As parents, we try so hard to reach our kids, to guide them and help them to live their best lives, but we often feel like we are hitting a brick wall. Getting encouragement and guidance from a tutor who believes in them and whom they think is amazing often provides a breakthrough.

When I discuss this often overlooked aspect of one-to-one tutoring with parents, their eyes light up at the thought of someone connecting with and impacting their child's life. The reward of seeing children's lives turn around with the help of a dedicated tutor is what makes my job so satisfying.

This brings to mind a Grade 9 student we had, whose parents called us to come for a consultation. This young man was a gentle hearted, sweet-tempered guy, but his reading skills were weak and his organizational skills were even weaker. He was barely passing his courses and the thought of moving up into more difficult ones with each grade was a daunting one for him. He felt discouraged, and 'stupid' and figured school just wasn't for him.

For him, school was just something to get through. His parents were frustrated and tried to help, but it rarely went well. When he got frustrated with something, he would simply push their buttons, and because they cared so much, their emotions quickly rose to the surface and an argument brought an end to the homework session. It was a vicious cycle that was causing the family daily stress, damaging the relationships, and only causing academics to be an even more taxing issue than it already was—a common story I hear all too often.

When I met with the family, my heart went out to them and I felt their pain. I knew they needed a mentor-type tutor. Not a brainiac, but rather, a good role model who was patient, kind and warm. We had just the right tutor for him and got them matched as soon as we could.

Within two months, the dreaded report cards were due and we all awaited their arrival with trepidation. He had gone from almost failing to getting C+s and Bs! Now, in two months, a tutor is not going to be able to change the student's conceptual understanding of grade level material that much, so what was the secret to his success?

The difference was helping him learn how to manage his studies, prepare for tests, complete assignments properly, and increase his confidence overall. He learned HOW to be a student and acquired those skills that every student needs to succeed in academics and in life. He wanted to impress his tutor because his tutor cared about and believed in him. When I saw his mom after the report card came, she ran up to me, threw her arms around me, and thanked me for turning things around for her son. That is the power of a mentor tutor.

Compensates for Learning Differences

> My tutor was an amazing person who showed me many different ways to tackle each math problem. He was patient, kind and very encouraging.
>
> —Kristi, Student

One-to-one tutoring compensates for learning differences and challenges. Everyone's brains are wired differently, but everyone can learn. However, we learn better if material is presented in a way that aligns with our dominant learning style. A student can compensate to suit a teacher's style, but even then, learning will be more effective if the information is delivered visually for a visual learning student, actively for a kinesthetic learner, or verbally for an auditory learner. (For some practical information on learning styles and how to adapt tutoring accordingly, do a search online or read Anne Crossman's *Study Smart, Study Less*.[32])

> *If the student does not understand, then the tutor will try a different approach until they 'get it.'*

When a tutor is working with a student, the tutor will check constantly that the student is keeping up and understanding the information that has been presented. Because the one-to-one setting allows for constant, active feedback, a tutor can quickly identify when a student is not absorbing the lesson. If the student does not understand, then the tutor will try a different approach until they 'get it.' This compensation process happens naturally in one-to-one tutoring. The student gets personalized attention and the tutor has time to stop, go back, break it down, explain it in a different way, or even go back to a previously missed building block. When we interview tutors, we notice that experienced tutors understand this and are skilled at trying different methods to present information to students.

This process rarely happens in a classroom situation, because information is most often presented at the front of a classroom, in an audio-linguistic format at a difficulty level that aligns with the middle of the classroom skill level. Students who are advanced are not challenged and remedial students get left behind. Teachers have a very difficult job juggling students who possess a wide range of skills. It is impossible for them to tailor every lesson to every level, need, or learning style. Often, large class sizes make it impossible for them to present information in a variety of ways or to cater to the needs of the disparate groups of students they have. Most often their efforts have to be aimed at classroom management. Teachers have a tough job!

Another consideration is students who have learning disabilities (LD). Many students struggle with these and, sadly, many go undiagnosed. Ironically, people with learning disabilities often have average or higher intelligence. There is the belief amongst some that LDs are the result of a unique brain structure[33]. Einstein is one of many famous and successful people to have had a learning disability.

> *We all have a unique brain with different strengths and weaknesses.*

I have noticed that, though higher-functioning autistic students may struggle with executive and people skills, they are often incredibly gifted in other areas, especially with numbers. The reality is that we all have a unique brain with different strengths and weaknesses. Learning to capitalize on our strengths and compensate for our weaknesses helps us to function in this world and jump through the hoops we all must negotiate to achieve our goals.

While it is not the tutor or educational consultant's role to diagnose a learning disability (in my opinion that should only be done by a professional who is trained to give psychological educational assessments), the tutoring process can support a student in areas of weakness and help them learn the skills they need to manage better.

When a student is lost, a good tutor will backtrack, try different ways, break the information down, get creative in their presentation, and check for understanding. They will patiently persist until the student understands the concept. They will also teach the student how to convert information into a format that suits the way they learn so that they can be independent learners. While an academic tutor can compensate for learning disabilities she or he is not a qualified therapist and will not 'fix' the situation.

However, through the assistance of the tutor, students will learn coping mechanisms, how to compensate for challenges, gain a better understanding of the material, and bolster their confidence. For many students, this is enough to help them 'learn how to learn', and manage their studies. It is important to note that serious learning disabilities will require a therapist and one-to-one tutoring is not enough. For these students, it is essential to get a professional assessment and recommendations for ongoing support.

A good example how one-to-one tutoring supports learning disabilities is the work we do with many autistic students. These students often are very bright and have no problem with the concepts in a class, but are very weak in the area of executive functioning. Executive function is the ability to engage in goal-directed activity, along with the mental processes that make this possible. Students on the autism spectrum often find it difficult to plan ahead, organize their study materials, complete assignments, or create a plan of attack for a larger project. We find that getting a tutor to provide some direction and support in these areas is often the big difference in helping these students be successful.

Tutor Match

> Tutor Doctor (on the first go) found my daughter the perfect tutor to match her learning style! We love that our tutor has a great sense of humor and many different teaching techniques to draw from (i.e. if my daughter doesn't understand something her tutor can teach it in a different way until she understands). She is very patient, thoughtful, knowledgeable, and flexible. We love the positive encouragement and immediate feedback.
>
> —Debra, Parent

When doing one-to-one tutoring you get to choose a tutor that matches not only a student's academic needs, but also their personality, learning style, schedule, location, and sometimes even interests! A great match can be a magical thing.

When a student looks up to their tutor, respects and likes them, there is a natural connection that makes communication easier, learning more fun and motivates a student to do the best they can. Some students need a tutor who is patient, encouraging, and gentle. While others need a tutor that can keep them on task and provide some accountability and organization. If you have a student who is a bit of a Chatty Cathy, you need a tutor who is focused, or they won't get anything done.

How many of us have had a teacher we just could not connect with? Inevitably a student in this situation will struggle with focusing in the class, lack motivation, and finish with a poor grade. When I do consultations with families I will ask about a student's previous and current grades. When there is one class that stands out as a poor grade I can almost always predict that the student 'didn't like' that teacher and some of the foundation learning has not taken place.

Conversely, if a student 'likes' their tutor, they will do better than they previously thought possible. We have seen this over and over again. I love it when we get a phone call from a parent telling us that their child 'thinks their tutor is cool' and looks forward to the tutoring session and has all the books out and ready for their session. Getting that right fit can make all the difference in helping get the breakthrough that we all want.

Efficient

> My son learns more in the one hour of one-to-one than he does in a week of the same subject in class at school.
>
> —Carolynn, Parent

One-to-one tutoring allows the tutor to focus on exactly what the student needs. If a parent wants their child to get caught up to grade level, the tutor can work through the coursework with the student. When they come across a concept that the student already understands, the tutor can skip it and move on. In a classroom situation, the student would just have to sit and wait for the teacher to finish that lesson and then do the homework, even though they had already mastered it. This wasted time and energy often causes a child to get frustrated, which can lead to behavior issues at home and at school. A personal tutor can move through the curriculum much more quickly and adapt the material for the student for faster understanding of the concepts involved.

Goal Alignment

> Our tutor has made a huge difference to my child's approach to math. She instills confidence and works with my child using identified strengths.
>
> —Diane, Parent

There are a lot of people who have particular needs that cannot be easily met in a classroom situation or can't even find classes that would help them meet their goals. An adult student who needs to improve their math grade to get into a program may not have the time to join a class or even have one available to join. A high-functioning autistic student may need help managing their time and coursework, but they don't have difficulty with the actual content of the course.

Many families are extremely busy and stressed and find that having a tutor come to provide homework help relieves conflict in the family and provides the expertise that helps a student succeed. When I do consultations, I write a full student profile and make clear goals for tutoring the specific student we will be working with. These goals are agreed upon with the parents, the teacher when possible, and then given to the tutor so everyone is on the same page.

For one little guy we enrolled, we had goals to 'increase his confidence, work on phonics skills, help him enjoy learning, communicate with his teacher, and have him reading at grade level by the start of the next school year.' For a Grade 9 student, we had the following goals: 'fill gaps in her foundational knowledge, support her with homework, and go over current curriculum. Ensure that assignments are planned for and time budgeted out. She would like a 'C+' this year for the sake of her confidence.' Every student is unique. Communicating with the student, parents, teachers, tutor, and any other professionals help us to work together to set the appropriate goals for a student and help them to reach them.

Targeted Instruction

> I have seen the changes first hand and see how important it is for our kids to not struggle through their classes, that they can actually enjoy school if they understand it.
>
> —Julie, Parent

One-to-one tutoring allows students to be taught at their current level of proficiency. In a classroom setting, the teacher has to teach to the middle of the class. If a student's skills are behind, then he is lost, and if a student's skills are ahead, then he is bored. In one-to-one tutoring, supplemental materials can be added at the student's level for those who are ahead of the class. For those who are struggling, time can be taken to ensure that a student understands a concept. If the student has not grasped the idea the tutor can explain it in another way until they understand.

On the other hand, we often have students come to us who have very aggressive goals. They want to get into a particular university or program, get scholarships, ace the ACT or the SAT, or get a very high 'A' average. Getting a one-to-one tutor ensures a different kind of mentorship for these students. If the student is in Physics, then we can get a Physics expert in to work with them and take them to a level of expertise in the subject that they couldn't have achieved on their own or through the teaching in their classroom.

A tutor who has already been successful in a subject can inspire, stretch, and help a student understand what is coming in future levels of the subject. In order to achieve such high marks, it is important to actually master the subject matter, which means going beyond what is in your grade level. Getting a personal tutor who is a subject expert helps these high-achieving and conscientious students reach their goals and do more than they could have with just hard work.

Materials

My newest student wrote his mid-term exam last Wednesday evening for his BSW (Janitorial) course. I was told by his aide to 'expect him to fail' and that he had pre-approval for a rewrite of the exam. When I heard those words, I replied, 'That is *not* acceptable to me,' and that I would work very hard with him to make sure he passes. I got a text message from his mom on Saturday night. We were both so ecstatic and proud of his hard work. He scored 95 percent!

—Belinda, Tutor

In a one-to-one teaching situation, you can work with whatever materials work for, or are needed, by the student. Some students work better on a computer than with paper and pen. For those students, an online curriculum is best. For other students the reverse is true. If a student needs to focus on phonics, then a phonics book can be supplemented. If the student is a homeschooler with their own unique curriculum, a tutor can work with that.

Many adult students are studying for a particular exam or program. We have tutored students for a security guard course, to pass a firefighter's exam, automotive training, and pretty much anything else you can think of; we just have to get the right tutor. A one-to-one tutor can adapt and work with whatever material needs to be covered.

Materials can also be chosen according to a student's strongest learning style. For a visual learner, visual curriculum and manipulatives are best. Part of setting up a student for success is assessing what materials are being used, must be used for a particular program, or need to be added. Then getting the right tutor to walk that student through those materials and adapt them to best meet that student's needs and goals.

Gaps in Learning

My tutor was very helpful in keeping me focused on my weak points and strengthening them.

—Jack, Student

A private tutor can take the time to fill the gaps in learning and work with where a student is actually at. Frequently we have had students who are quite behind for their grade level; sometimes two or three years. For a student like this, the classroom situation is quite frustrating because the material in class is going completely over their head. When we enroll this type of student, we work to find materials appropriate for that student's level. This way the student receives instruction appropriate to where she or he is at so that building blocks are not missed and the student can be brought up to grade level and can then manage to keep up in class.

Over the years it's become clear to me that most students don't learn the basics skills in *how* to be a good student. They have not learned time management, organizational skills, or effective study methods. Often their backpacks, lockers, and binders look like the hapless victims of an explosion and rarely do we run across an actual organizational system. Most students struggle with a lack of focus, procrastinating, getting frustrated, and basically avoiding their work. Usually, the first thing the tutor needs to do is to pull out the backpack and binder and get the student organized. Then the tutor needs to create a system for prioritizing and managing tasks. Chapter 4.1 of this book covers this well, so please refer to that chapter for further information.

Whatever gaps a student is struggling with, one-to-one tutoring provides the opportunity to focus on these issues and fill them in so the student can be successful.

Conclusion

Education has seen a trend towards individualization of instruction. *Forbes* magazine listed Personalization as one of the top four trends in education. According to Forbes, learning is being optimized in terms of different learning styles and the experiences of individuals, largely due to technology and other similar resources.[34] The emergence of flipped classrooms, MOOCs (Massive Online Open Courses), self-paced programs and curricula, and the growth of homeschooling, are a result of this growing desire to meet individual needs. One-to-one tutoring allows for complete individualization of support materials, goals, teaching method/style, and focus. Where one-to-one instruction is possible, we can achieve far more in terms of student understanding, motivation, and success.

This reality is very well demonstrated by one particular young boy that I enrolled. He was in a very bad place when I initially met him at the consultation with his mom. He had no joy for learning, was shutting down and withdrawing, and had to be "dragged by the ankles" to get him to go to school. One year later, by matching him with the right tutor and support materials, he has completely changed. He is joyful, able to express himself, has discovered new tactics for learning that work for him, and is able to interpret information. He loves the tutoring process, is receiving teaching at his level and is inspired to tackle new levels. According to his mom Angela, "The tutor matching, teaching methods, and adaption of materials has really worked for him. There is no comparison between the mass manufactured approach to education that churns kids through a system vs the customized, individualized and undivided attention he receives with this approach."

The power of one-to-one tutoring is really in the potential outcomes a student will see. With this model, the ability to change a student's motivation, competencies, and potential is completely possible.

3.2 Learning for Life

By Gavin Hopper

Gavin has worked in the education sector as a teacher in Japan and later in administration/marketing for 15 years. He is an experienced international education marketing professional, presents on marketing related topics at international conferences and assists his clients from government to the private sector about education marketing trends.

Lifelong learning is about so much more than just simply learning to pass required exams to move on to the next level. It is not to simply make your parents proud, or your teachers happy or even keeping your employers pleased. It is about learning new ideas and gaining an understanding of different concepts and topics throughout your entire life. When we commit to lifelong learning, we are committing to progressing and furthering our own personal and professional development. It involves learning that has a purpose and a meaning; learning that makes a person a better-rounded citizen, and learning that benefits your entire community in so many ways. Sir John Monash, a decorated First World War Australian Military commander once said: "Adopt as your fundamental creed that you will equip yourself for life, not solely for your own benefit but for the benefit of the whole community."

So, it's not only our children who should focus on learning. As parents, teachers, and mentors, it is up to us to not only act as an example but to learn new approaches and philosophies. Not only are we an example, learning beyond our school years can make life more interesting than we can imagine.

While I am from Melbourne, Australia, I know that these learnings are universal. In fact, I conducted a worldwide survey on what I call "Learning for Life", and there were a lot of interesting results. I have put together what I found to be the most thought-provoking and relevant to what learning for life really means.

What is Learning for Life?

1. A lifelong learning perspective is more than training and continuing education: it forces us to rethink and reinvent our schools and universities.[35,36]

2. Learning for life should benefit the community and the environment.

As the meaning of Learning for Life does not have an exact precise definition and is conceptual, I have chosen two of my favorite quotes on the topic of education, learning, and life. Firstly, "Wisdom is not a product of schooling but of the lifelong attempt to acquire it," from Albert Einstein. Secondly, "Live as if you were to die tomorrow. Learn as if you were to live forever." This comes to us from Mahatma Gandhi.

Learning for life is not just about academic learning. It is about the many skills we acquire throughout our lives. Such as communication — from the written word to verbal interaction, and knowing how to listen to others. These are all skills required in everyday life. To be productive members of society, we all need to learn how to interact with others, whether it is in an academic or professional environment, or even just personal relationships.

Nick Founder is thirty-six years of age. He is a lawyer from Melbourne, Australia, and author of *Finding True Friends*. He believes that "Learning for Life" is a holistic experience and involves learning from numerous sources. In his case, he has learned many cultural traditions from his Greek and Chinese family. He has developed numeracy skills as well as verbal and written communication skills. Also, Nick has a better understanding of economics, law and writing through his schooling and university studies. Other skills acquired include: being practical, negotiation and problem solving through interaction with managers and mentors in various jobs. While these are all important to his everyday life, Nick believes the greatest skills he has learned are writing, communication and being able to collaborate with others. These allow him to function more effectively and definitely help his ability to continue his learning. His biggest challenge has been working with people whose work methodologies and personalities differ from his own and being innovative in, for example, legal and business scenarios. Nick is currently studying towards a master's degree in writing and is considering a PhD in creative writing.

The Lifelong Learning Council of Queensland describes four "pillars" of learning for life:

- **Learning to know** — mastering learning tools rather than acquisition of structured knowledge.

- **Learning to do** — equipping people for the types of work needed now and in the future including innovation and adaptation of learning to future work environments.

- **Learning to live together, and with others** — peacefully resolving conflict, discovering other people and their cultures, fostering community capability, individual competence and capacity, economic resilience, and social inclusion.

- **Learning to be** — education contributing to a person's complete development: mind and body, intelligence, sensitivity, aesthetic appreciation, and spirituality.

Learning on the Job

What about work? It is where we spend a good chunk of our lives after all. Well, the workplace is an excellent Learning for Life tool as well. Lifelong education involves facilitating learning on the job and creating a culture to motivate (potential) learners. For example, the workplace teaches employees and employers what it means to have a solid work ethic. This is imperative if you want to excel and move forward in the professional ranks or hierarchy. The workplace also teaches us about Occupational Health and Safety rules and regulations. Why is this important? It means that all workers are doing their required job/tasks in a safe and secure environment, which is imperative to fostering a culture of learning. You can't be focused on educating yourself if you fear for your safety. A more obvious— but no less important—learning benefit from the job is learning to be more organized. Organization not only allows us to operate more effectively, but it also teaches us to prioritize. It is also about learning objectivity when dealing with problem-solving situations. The list of learning benefits from the workplace goes on and on: learning to think positively, setting goals, acquiring administrative skills, paying attention to detail, being able to think analytically, and learning how to do proper research. What's clear is that all of these skills are transferable to everyday life, and they are skills we are never done honing.

We also can't forget about innovation and technology. Innovation can benefit businesses, employees, and the community at large and is an important part of Learning for Life. So, it is very important to keep up with changing technology and other developments in a rapidly changing globalized economy, whether on the job or at home. Technology is changing at such a rapid rate that we must constantly keep ourselves updated. By the time you read this, we'll probably be on to the iPhone 9, which will be capable of projecting a hologram of you anywhere in the world. Maybe. There are, however, some challenges in achieving greater participation in learning for life across all levels of society. A lot of people have difficulty under-standing or using new technology, particularly older individuals who were not raised with computers and smartphones. Others may not be able to find the time needed to really master their chosen technol-ogy, especially if what they want to learn is in an area outside of their current employment and requires after-hours learning, often juggled with family and other responsibilities. And let's be honest, there is also the belief that Learning for Life is boring because they have not found a type of learning that is interesting or relevant to them or been able to find a method that is appropriate for them and their circumstances.

Gerhard Fischer[37] states there are two essential skill sets that will remain at the top of the list of job requirements for twenty-first-century work. First is the ability to quickly acquire and apply new knowledge. Second is the know-how to apply the essential twenty-first-century skills of problem-solving, communication, teamwork, technology use and innovation. We live in a knowledge and information economy where the required knowledge in a given job is constantly changing and evolving with technology.

The authors Aspin and Chapman in their book *Lifelong Learning Concepts and Conceptions,*[38] believe that the central elements of lifelong learning are economic progress and development; personal development and fulfillment; and social inclusiveness and democratic understanding and activity. I tend to agree with them. Learning can either be for internal gratification or external. An example is workplace development. It seems many people would feel the same way. One survey respondent, Paresh K, a business analyst from Melbourne, Australia, shares the opinion that learning for life is about "being open to discovering and learning news ideas, concepts, and topics throughout your life."

> *"You cannot open a book without learning something."* — *Confucius*

Learning for Life skills are acquired in many ways throughout one's life. Firstly, there is the formal structured higher education through primary, secondary, and tertiary studies. There is also on the job training and experience as an employee or through one's own business enterprise. Learning through a mentor can also be beneficial, whether the mentor is a friend, family member, colleague, business associate or even someone you pay to be a professional mentor. What about travel experiences? When we are out of our normal everyday familiar environment, we are forced to learn and adapt to new settings and people, and to learn from new experiences. Reading, whether an academic text or a novel for recreational purposes is one of the best aids in Life Learning. And don't forget about online resources. They are also a great learning tool; from searching the World Wide Web to watching and browsing through YouTube videos. Neil Armstrong states that "Research is creating new knowledge." We can also learn a lot from our peers and loved ones and social environment and the list goes on and on. To put it into simple terms, we never stop learning. Different situations and scenarios allow us to always continue to learn and develop new ideas. Learning for Life is an ongoing process.

> *"Tell me and I forget. Teach me and I remember. Involve me and I learn."* — *Xunzi*

Learning for Life also involves developing psychological skills, which we need when dealing with and managing relationships, whether they are personal, academic, physical, parental, or professional. Activities such as participating in group sports can teach us fair play, to be participating as part of a team and teaches us physical contact skills as well. Even dancing can help further develop and refine these skills. Cooking teaches us to follow methodology and instruction and cleaning and gardening also help us to acquire life skills. Solo life experiences such as meditation are all learning tools to help support an individual's emotional, spiritual growth and well-being. When there is life experience, we are better able to cope with detrimental issues such as stress, loss, abuse, bullying, health and financial issues. As Henry Ford stated, "Life is a series of experiences, each one of which makes us bigger, even though sometimes it is hard to realize this. For the world was built to develop character, and we must learn that the setbacks and grieves which we endure help us in our marching onward."

Why is Learning for Life Beneficial?

The Singaporean Minister for Education, Minister Heng Swee Keat, echoed the words of Sir John Monash in a parliamentary speech dated March 6, 2015, where he discussed how Singapore built up its education system and in doing so, grew its economy. He argued against a 'study book' culture, namely where success is largely measured by academic grades. He went on to emphasize the importance of holistic self-directed learning and soft skills such as creativity, inventiveness, adaptability, socio-emotional skills, and cultural and global awareness. Minister Heng Swee Keat cautioned against churning out students who excel in examinations but are ill-equipped to take on jobs of the future, nor find fulfillment in what they do. He referred to holistic learning for life as mastery learning and emphasized the need for mastery learning in every field.

Again, what about the workplace? Learning for Life is beneficial in the workplace as upskilling can lead employees to a higher promotion and in turn, better pay and conditions. As a result, they will be more satisfied, fulfilled and overall, happier workers that feel appreciated. And a happier employee generally improves productivity, so it's a win/win. Upskilling can also lead to new opportunities including potential self-employment opportunities in the future. Alexis M., a forty-six-year-old payroll manager in Malaysia, stated that 'Learning for Life' involves learning every day for your whole life; that learning organizational skills has been important for her in busy payroll, accounts, and administration roles.

Learning for Life in Practice

It is interesting to consider that employers like PricewaterhouseCoopers (PWC)—the multinational, professional services firm—is blacking out certain details from CVs (including school and university details) to avoid bias in hiring. The fact that such a policy is being implemented on the one hand suggests that there is a bias with many employers in favor of which university a candidate went to and what their grades were. On the other hand, it shows a shift by industry perhaps to look at more than just qualifications in hiring a candidate. This is an approach more in line with Learning for Life, where a multitude of skills is considered important.

An acquaintance of mine, John, who is in his mid-thirties with a family and living in a well-to-do suburb of Sydney, Australia, was telling me that his Taiwanese father was always insistent on him doing as much higher education as possible, preferably up to the PhD level. John's father had worked mainly for leading universities and even the United Nations at one point. However, while John did study for a master's degree, he found it did not put him where he wanted to be in life and career. Several years ago, John decided to do some hands-on work and left the finance profession to work as a mortgage broker for a home loan company. In doing so, John developed on the job skills that he did not acquire in any of his university studies. Eventually, John started his own successful mortgage broking business, and he still tells his father that Learning for Life is so much more than a university education.

> *I try to encourage my tutors to embrace holistic learning.*

I have noticed in recent times through dealings with universities and colleges in Australia, that the old model of learning only through expensive prescribed textbooks, is giving way to learning that involves practical placements within relevant industry and modern techniques, such as online study. Having said that, I deal with many parents who are resistant to the new methods of teaching. When they were in school or university, they were used to standardized tests. However, it's about showing them a new, more effective path. I try to encourage my tutors to embrace holistic learning if they are not doing so already because in my view problem solving, reasoning, analytic skills, communication, teamwork, and adaptability are all absolutely essential in the twenty-first-century learning that is connected to Learning for Life. They can come from academic institutions such as secondary schools and universities, both of which offer a more formal structured education, or even on the job training. The avenue doesn't matter, it's about the fact that you're learning.

Socializing is also a great tool for Learning for Life. Celebrating with good friends and loved ones as well as getting to know new acquaintances, creates many life-changing and memorable experiences. When spending time with others, we can develop self-awareness, learn to deal with different social situations and even get some feedback from our peers. Having social experiences can make us more tolerant towards other individuals, more forgiving, more respectful, more understanding, and we can even learn from one another. Anna S., a thirty-six-year-old PhD candidate from Canberra said, Learning for Life includes lessons and skills that she can transfer to different parts of her life. Anna stated that life skills she has acquired include public speaking, cooking (through watching her mum and advice from friends), and meditation. Bringing it closer to home is my own mother, who is sixty-five and retired, from Melbourne, Australia, who stated that Learning for Life involves gaining more knowledge from other people and books. One of her greatest challenges in learning has been around maintaining a positive attitude in relationships and business dealings.

As an education facilitator, my values in terms of Learning for Life are that I believe in the unlimited potential of the individual. I believe that relationships need mutual respect and integrity. We must approach the world with a determined curiosity, not just looking for new answers but also for new questions. We must always look for ways to evolve and improve, self-reflect and to also learn from failure, not letting failure beat us. We must all be accountable for our actions and learn from them, owning our part, and overcoming obstacles and trying to obtain the results we so desperately desire. Learning for Life involves making a contribution to others and trying to make a difference in some way, in any way. It is having a commitment to innovation, to be a positive part of a team, a team player and to accomplish a revolutionary vision.

The Survey

In the survey, I asked:

1. What do you understand is the meaning of the phrase "Learning for Life" in one or two sentences?

2. Name two or three life skills and how you acquired them? (e.g.: at school; university; at work; online learning; reading)

3. What has been your greatest learning challenge in life and how did you overcome it?

4. What plans do you have for your future learning?

> *Perseverance is very important because life involves challenges, whether at work, in relationships, or with health.*

The respondent was Alessandra DeSouza. Alessandra is thirty-seven years of age, a lawyer and a teacher who is from Sao Paulo, Brazil. She stated that Learning for Life includes learning skills such as standing up for yourself and not giving up. She has learned skills such as perseverance and tolerance, as well as how to study and work efficiently and be organized. Her greatest learning challenge has been to see problems in an objective way, notwithstanding having studied law at university. She believes that perseverance is very important because life involves challenges, whether at work, in relationships, or with health. Alessandra believes in being proactive and not just letting life happen to you and blaming other people for things that go wrong. She wishes to improve her future learning by undertaking courses available through her work.

The second was a young man by the name of Nathaniel Beaumont. Nathaniel is twenty-six and works as a child care worker, as well as being a student in Melbourne, Australia. He said that Learning for Life to him means to learn something new in whatever capacity, whether it is formal learning, on the job learning or learning a language or new craft. He notes that the most important time in one's life for learning is at the ages of about zero to five. Nathaniel went on to say how he had learned some Greek from his stepdad and also Spanish at an adult learning night class. He has also learned cooking through his mother who was a chef before retirement. One of his biggest learning challenges has been dealing with negative or difficult people. In future, he wishes to be a politician and wants to learn from mentoring, in addition to studying politics at university.

We live in a very different world compared to the past centuries. Quite often, up until say the 1970s, a person went to school and studied very generic topics that had little practical application. Students were required to rote learn and a failure to do so could result in severe punishment. As Martin Farquhar Tupper said: "Memory is not wisdom; idiots can by rote repeat volumes. Yet what is wisdom without memory?"

Even still, graduating was not necessarily expected, especially if the economic situation at home was dire and money was needed for immediate economic survival. So many would do a job that was "physical", from the day they left school until retirement. However, even these more physical jobs have changed in our current society. In today's world, a very good example would be that even a "hands-on" crash repairer must keep up to date with technology to remain competitive.

In the pre-1970s, higher education numbers were fairly low. The degree you earned did not have to be useful or competitive because you were in an elite group. Nowadays, using law graduates as an example, up to 50 percent of those graduates do not attain jobs in the legal field. At the moment, Australia has around 60 thousand practicing lawyers and 30 thousand graduates each year. There are often 100 applications for every one law job. There are more university places than jobs. So which law graduates are attaining the jobs? Given that some large employers are changing their hiring practices to black out a student's university and grades, it comes down to other skills. What skills are they? Well, the ones you need to succeed in life, whatever your chosen field, be it professional, a trade or as a businessperson.

Failure to embrace Learning for Life could affect economic growth through lack of innovation and inefficiencies in employment and business. "He who learns but does not think, is lost! He who thinks but does not learn is in great danger," was a great quote by Confucius. Out of date skills can lead to inefficiencies in business and loss of profit, affecting the general economy. Social, technological, and environmental benefits to society may not be realized. As Peter Drucker said, "Innovation is the specific instrument of entrepreneurship ... the act that endows resources with a new capacity to create wealth." We all must embrace Learning for Life as it is crucial for economic growth and success.

> *Learning for Life is about learning for your own life and not someone else's.*

My eleven-year-old son is not yet sure what he wants to do when he finishes school. However, I know many people who were pushed by their parents to study Law or Medicine upon finishing secondary school. In some cases, it worked out well, but in others, it has led to great unhappiness. In this situation, if a person has internal unhappiness or does not feel fulfilled completely or satisfied, it can lead to feelings of disillusionment, depression and often feeling as though they have failed in their lives. Learning for Life is about learning for your own life and not someone else's. The future is yours to make of it what you desire, what will bring you the most fulfillment and joy in your life. That's why I said to my son, "Do something that will suit your personality and your skills, but most importantly, do something that you will be happy doing."

I would like to dedicate this chapter to my eleven-year-old son. He will finish school in the early 2020s. It is absolutely a time of wonderment and excitement, yet I would even suggest possibly a more difficult time than when I finished school. Son, always keep in mind that when you finish school, it's not the end of your learning, it's simply the beginning. Do not worry at 18 if you don't know what you want to do for the rest of your life, many of us did not. There are many avenues out there to explore if you need to. It is all part of learning. If you think you have found your passion already at 18, then absolutely look forward and go for it. To borrow words from Sir John Monash to end on, "Equip yourself for life, not solely for your own benefit but for the benefit of the whole community."

4. The Power of Change

4.1 Better Organized: Better Grades

By Bob Rosedale

Colonel (Ret'd) Bob Rosedale is Vice President of Operations for Tutor Doctor. Bob retired from the U.S. Air Force (USAF) after a twenty-six year career of distinguished service in a variety of assignments both in the U.S. and abroad. He holds the rating of Command Pilot and served as the United States Defense Attaché at the U.S. Embassy, Riyadh, Saudi Arabia, followed by a second diplomatic tour as the Air Attaché assigned to the U.S. Embassy in Madrid, Spain. Upon retiring from the Air Force, Bob and his wife Sylvia arrived in the Boise/Treasure Valley area to pursue their passion for helping students achieve academic success, build self-confidence, and prepare themselves for all of life's challenges.

A few months ago I was asked to write a chapter for a new Tutor Doctor book about how students undermine their success due to an inability to manage their time, stay focused on high priority tasks, and organize their lives to be successful. For some reason, the home office at Tutor Doctor thought that, since I was the author of their Academic Game Plan (AGP), I would be well-suited for this endeavor.

Fueled primarily by my own ego, I found this to be an exciting opportunity and enthusiastically agreed ... but then got distracted with running my Tutor Doctor franchise and forgot to write the chapter. A few weeks later, I received a reminder that it was due in about twenty-one days, so I hunkered down and wrote. I was very proud of my work but lost it before I had a chance to turn it in to my editor. Actually, I didn't lose the article — it was still on my laptop and over the years, I've learned to "save" often — I just lost the computer.

This seems to happen to me all the time. I set out with great intentions, occasionally finish what I start, and invariably fail to reach the goals that I set out for myself in the first place. This is frustrating but I'm great at rationalizing my own failure, so I tell people it's just who I am and there's probably nothing I can do about it. In fact, people should stop expecting so much from me or they will live a life of stress, disappointment, and frustration themselves.

On the other hand, while I was looking for the laptop, I did find a discount coupon for 50 percent off a round of golf that I had paid a hefty price for at a silent auction but had misplaced earlier this year. Unfortunately, it expired last week.

As you can see I might not be the best person to write this article. Or, maybe I am. When it comes to organizing our lives, completing our highest priority tasks, and proactively managing our time, most of us are somewhat inconsistent ... especially students. Let me give you an example:

About three years ago I was asked to visit a home one evening to provide an education consultation for a family with a sixteen-year-old boy who was, by all standards, a "genius". He had never failed anything in his life and maintained a straight 'A' average throughout his home-school curriculum. The reason the parents requested the consultation was because he had enrolled in an online calculus class at the beginning of the year and within a few weeks was failing it miserably. Since Mom wasn't the right person to help him with calculus, the family decided to seek out one-to-one tutoring to help get their son back on track in the online course.

Smart But Scattered

From my perspective, this was a pretty straightforward enrollment. I had plenty of excellent calculus tutors and it was merely a matter of selecting the one who I felt would be the best match for the young man. We use the "whole person" concept to facilitate the best match possible, so I began asking him a few questions about his extracurricular interests, hobbies, and goals. One of the questions I asked him was, "Are you a Boy Scout?" to which he replied enthusiastically:

"Yes, scouting is very important in our family and goes back generations." When I heard this, I responded, "Well, you must be an Eagle Scout by now, right?" There was a slight pause and silence at the table and the boy's shoulders dropped a little. Before he could answer, his father interjected. In fact, these were the first words the father spoke during the entire consultation. What he said though, changed the course of how I approach working with students, as well as the trajectory of countless students after his son.

What the father said was, "No, my son is not an Eagle Scout and that is disappointing for him and the rest of the family." Now, the father didn't say this in a mean-spirited or in a criticizing manner. He said it rather matter-of-factly and followed it by explaining, "Bob, I've been listening to everything you have recommended and it all makes perfect sense, except for one thing: my son doesn't need a math tutor. He didn't fail the online course because he can't understand math. My son has a 150 IQ and can do the math. He failed the course for the same reason he is not an Eagle Scout ... and now that I think about it, I don't want a math tutor in my house."

Well, for a guy who didn't speak very much, he sure said some interesting things when he did. Ostensibly, calculus was the problem, and the solution for the dad was no math tutor in his house. So, I asked the father what he had in mind. He responded, "I want someone who will help my son be successful in *everything* he does, not just teach him math. My son failed the online course because he couldn't organize his time on his own. He gets distracted by shiny objects. He doesn't know how to prioritize tasks or manage his time. As a homeschooler, for 11 years his mother has been making sure he gets everything done and stays on task, but he's leaving for college in 18 months and frankly, we're all a little scared to death that he won't be able to manage his time to be successful in that environment. So, what I want from you is someone who can coach my son on how to develop these skills. I don't know what to call them, but that's what I want. The question is can you provide that?"

I responded to the father with the same response I always use when I have no idea what I'm going to do: "Gimme two weeks. If you can give me two weeks, I'll be able to do one of three things: (1) propose a solution, (2) ask for a little more time or (3) tell you I won't be able to help after all." We ended up going with option 1 and I'm happy to say that we were able to coach him through all of the challenges.

After that consultation, a funny thing happened: I started to hear versions of the same concerns all the time—especially from parents of middle and high school students. They all were frustrated because they felt their children had the aptitude to achieve whatever they set their mind to, but they didn't execute on that for reasons beyond the parent's ability to easily describe or influence. Then, I started asking other Tutor Doctor franchise owners if they were hearing similar comments at their consultations. Across the board, they all told me that they are routinely inundated with inquiries from desperate parents who have children that are "smart, but scattered." They know that their children are capable, but they just aren't fulfilling their potential. This kind of behavior places an enormous amount of stress on both the student and on their families. Parents spend their time nagging for homework to be done because task initiation is part of having academic discipline.

Teachers will concur; they can see that the child has the ability to do well, but they just can't seem to turn in their work or stay focused in class. They routinely forget assignments and tests, and never leave enough time to study or complete assignments. They never get to show their true abilities while they are pulling all-nighters before exams or scrambling to complete assignments at the last minute.

Finally, students become stressed because they are always putting out fires, and poor time management means they never have enough time to do all they need to be successful students. As their grades suffer, they become even more frustrated because they know they can master the content, but they just don't seem to be able to pull it all together. All of this stress and tension in the home can't help but to negatively impact the student's confidence which, in turn, has even more negative repercussions on their performance.

Executive Function Deficit and How to Overcome It

After a few months observing this trend, I started to do some research, consulted with some experienced educators, and learned that what was going on was that these students were manifesting a deficit in what are clinically known as "executive functions". A lot has been written on executive functions in the past few years. In particular, I learned a tremendous amount on the subject from books like *Smart But Scattered* and *Smart But Scattered Teens*, by authors Richard Guare and Peg Dawson.[39] But the one piece of research literature that caught my attention the most was called *The Forgotten Middle Study* by the folks who created the ACT. This study set out to identify which factors provided the best indication of college or career readiness after high school. The conclusion they came to was that what students achieve academically by eighth grade has a bigger impact on their college and career preparation than their high school academic career.[40] To go further, not only was eighth grade academic achievement determined to be the best predictor of success, no other factor even came close to the predictive power of eighth grade academic achievement.

"What?" I asked myself. You mean high school academic performance doesn't predict success after high school? According to *The Forgotten Middle Study*, not in any measurable amount and here's why: it's because success after high school is more dependent on academic discipline than academic knowledge. What ends up happening is that, if a student hasn't sufficiently developed the skills that contribute to academic discipline by the time they complete middle school, then they find themselves falling behind, struggling, or not being able to keep all the plates spinning in high school and beyond.

This can even manifest itself in students who have always been at the top of their class until they started high school. My observation has been that, as long as the academic content up through eighth grade didn't really challenge the student, then they outperformed and they had no reason to develop time management and organizational skills. However, once these same students are challenged with multiple AP classes, along with numerous extracurricular activities, they simply don't possess the time management, prioritization, and organizational skills to be successful.

The bottom line is that clearly there are two components to academic success: academic foundations and academic discipline. All students need some balance of both, but no two students are the same. This realization is what led to the development of Tutor Doctor's X-Skills Game Plan.

Working with Tutor Doctor, I know the whole company is committed to increasing student confidence in the classroom so they can sustain their performance at higher and higher levels. The challenge we faced was how to efficiently support students in both the traditional area of academic foundation building—math, science, English, reading, and so on, as well as, develop the executive skills that can help students with their academic discipline. One thing I learned in the U.S. Air Force is that organization is obviously paramount. This is exactly what the X-Skills Game Plan does– it is a tool that we integrate into all of our enrollments (middle school and above) to help students develop their organizational and time management skills, as well as how to start thinking more strategically and proactively about their own learning. The tool is based on goal-directed persistence and incorporates concepts that I learned and instructed as a pilot in the U.S. Air Force. In the Air Force, we use terms like mission planning, pre-brief, debrief, checklist discipline, contingency planning, situational awareness and "staying ahead of the jet." Students can benefit from all of these concepts by using step-by-step, straightforward processes to plan their week in advance, write down and prioritize their most important tasks, consider the obstacles that might cause them to fail (better known as "excuses"), and identify resources required to be successful (no more sending Mom to Walmart at midnight for a piece of poster board!). When they're done, they've not only planned their week, they've planned their success.

How to Make Your Own Game Plan

Making your own game plan is just as simple and can be accomplished with a standard day-planner type calendar. The key steps are to first prep the calendar on Sunday evening by building an outline of the upcoming week's activities. Then, during the school day, the student needs to capture those high priority tasks that must be accomplished to step the student closer and closer to their academic goals—we call these Alpha tasks because they must be accomplished to achieve the most important or "Alpha" goal. A good technique is for the student to simply carry a colored index card to school every day and use it to capture each Alpha task as it is assigned, along with the date due. These are the only two pieces of information that need to be captured during the school day. Everything else can be done after the student comes home for the evening. The student can also make a list of important tasks or activities that need to be considered, yet are not vital for academic success. We call these "Beta" tasks. Finally, create a "Before Departing School" checklist on a second colored index card. I recommend laminating the card. It is critical that your student physically read this checklist every day before leaving school—if they try to run it from memory they are likely to fail. The back side of this card is a great place to write down the "Before School" checklist, which will ensure the student doesn't forget to take their completed assignments back to school after they've completed them.

Once the student gets home and has some free time after school, they need to do a few things with their list of Alpha Tasks. First, identify a date to complete each task that provides time to finish it, yet is flexible enough that they are not waiting until the last minute. Second, determine how long they anticipate it will take to accomplish each task and write it down. They also need to take some time to think about any obstacles that will prevent them from accomplishing an Alpha Task by the date they selected to complete it. Finally, write down any resources they need to be successful. As a parent, these last two items are critical to anticipate, as they comprise the bulk of the excuses students will turn to when they fail to accomplish their Alpha Tasks.

All that needs to be done now is to transfer the Alpha Task to a day-planner type calendar on the date it is actually due, followed by a second entry that blocks out the day and time the student has scheduled to complete the Alpha Task.

There is one more two-step technique that is designed to make it very easy for students and parents to maintain visibility not only on this week's priorities but for the other weeks and months as well. First, color code the student's classes. Second, whenever an Alpha Task is due beyond the current week, take a colored tab corresponding to the respective class and place it at the top of the page over the actual date it's due. As the semester unfolds, a rainbow will emerge that lets everyone know there are mid- and long-term tasks out there, which must be planned for early.

These are the basics of a rudimentary Tutor Doctor X-Skills Game Plan. The process isn't complicated, however, it does require reinforcement and follow-through to be effective. For our clients, the tutor coaches the student through this process at the beginning of each session. Parents can do the same thing or act as accountability coaches by reviewing the student's plan at the end of each day.

What Does Success Look Like?

So what does it mean to be successful in the first place? How do we define it in the context of the classroom? How would you personally define success for your child? Is it getting that 'A' grade? Being captain of the football team? Or, perhaps becoming an Eagle Scout? My definition of academic success is when a student is able to confidently sustain their performance at higher and higher levels. I particularly like this definition because I strongly believe that it captures the essence of self-motivation. As students gain confidence at higher and higher levels, it will be their natural inclination to seek out greater challenges throughout their academic career and their lives.

So, how do we get there from here? How do we provide a support structure that achieves success?

On the academic foundation building side, we're talking about the content that students learn in the classroom—most importantly, the foundational elements. To use a sports analogy, it's all about "fundamentals, fundamentals, fundamentals!" As athletes master the rules of the game, fundamental techniques, and basic strategies, they begin to gain the confidence they need to play the game successfully. As they gain more experience, they learn to confidently integrate more complex concepts and execute them at higher and higher levels. Incrementally, the commitment, perseverance, and practice cause the athlete's situational awareness to expand and they are able to, not only anticipate challenges but create strategies to overcome them. Most importantly, they become willing to take the calculated risks they need to be successful at the next level. They aren't comfortable beating the same competition they dominated last year—they seek out the next level of challenge. "Enough about athletes" you might say, "we're supposed to be talking about academics!"

Well, I am. Sports and academics share a very important feature—they are both performance-related activities that rely on confidence to be successful. Change the name of the game from basketball or football to Algebra and everything I just described is still 100 percent true ... and the most efficient way to accelerate an individual's development in this sport called Algebra is the same as any other sport—bring in a great coach (aka "tutor") who can motivate them, challenge them, and push them to work a little harder than they might want to work themselves.

Academic discipline is a little more elusive as it includes time management, organizational skills, sustained attention, following through on tasks, and working memory. To address this side of the Academic Success Formula we created the Tutor Doctor X-Skills Game Plan.

The X-Skills Game Plan is a straightforward, calendar-based agenda which incorporates a specific process to capture all of a student's tasks in a prioritized manner, develop a workable plan to execute all of those tasks and provide accountability for the student to follow throughout the week. It incorporates daily checklists to ensure students are prepared for each school day, as well as to make sure they are prepared to get their work done after school. At the end of each day, students are expected to provide an accountability debrief to their academic coach or parent, as well as, at the end of each week. The ultimate objective is to keep the student actively engaged on a day-to-day basis so they are actively assessing progress towards their goals.

Even though I have used the term "calendar-based agenda" to provide some context, it is important to understand that it is not the same as the school-issued agendas that most families are familiar with and which historically don't work. Most agendas are overly-expensive, glorified calendars—perhaps with pictures of the periodic table and a cutaway of the anatomy. However, they have no process associated with them and because students have no idea of what to do with the agenda, they are ineffective at helping them to be more organized. They also do not provide any features to hold students accountable. On the other hand, it's precisely these process elements that differentiate the X-Skills Game Plan from the typical agendas students receive from their schools.

But I Don't Need Your Game Plan

Interestingly, something else that doesn't work well for most students (or adults for that matter) is mobile devices and smartphones.

A great example of this was a young lady whom we started working with as a sophomore. She was extremely bright, attended an elite high school that provided a baccalaureate academic experience, and participated in many activities—most notably, debate. In fact, she seemed to like to practice her debate skills as often as possible, including during my initial consultation with the family where she articulated many fine arguments describing how she didn't need the Game Plan to organize her life. Rather, all she needed was her mobile phone and all of its built-in gadgetry. So, I asked her to show me what high priority tasks she had in her phone that were due this week, as well as what was coming up beyond this week and prior to the end of the semester. I also asked her to show me her plan to get it all done and I gave her 30 seconds to do all that. By the time the 30 seconds were up, she had just gotten past entering her password into the home screen. Once she did, she couldn't tell me anything about her plan to get all of her high-priority tasks completed. Clearly, the mobile phone wasn't helping her stay organized; although, it did give her a false sense of security that she had everything under control.

This was an amusing exercise (at least for me) that I used to make a point: mobile devices don't necessarily work well for helping people develop executive skills. I've rarely seen them work well for students. I suspect there are many reasons for this, but mostly I know why my smartphone doesn't work well for me other than to remind me of what's on the calendar.

For me, when the screen goes dark, my mind goes with it. What I mean by this is that the prioritized tasks lose their priority and importance. The context also disappears, which results in my losing visibility and situational awareness of the big picture. It's also too easy to simply "punch off" the reminders as they come flying in. I used to claim that smartphones weren't smart enough to tell me which obstacles would prevent me from carrying out a task or to proactively assign due dates that would allow me to create contingency plans. However, in the few years since I've been studying executive functions, dozens of applications have come on the market designed to do exactly these things. Interestingly, every time I try one, it doesn't seem to work for very long. Just like a kid with a new toy, each new application's utility fades away as quickly as I got excited about using it. I've come to the conclusion that I personally need something real and tangible, not "cool" and virtual—and I think many students are the same way.

What does work well is when we integrate an academic game plan into a tutoring enrollment. Whenever we are working with middle school students and above, our in-home tutors spend about 15 minutes each session reviewing the student's academic plan and coaching students to ensure that they are using a game plan and doing so correctly, as well as to provide insight on how the student might improve on a week-to-week basis. As students gain proficiency using the Game Plan correctly, families can look forward to three primary benefits:

1. Students will develop the necessary skills to execute tasks independently and achieve academic discipline, which means they will complete tasks on time and will be more organized. They will feel like they have more time in their lives to get everything done.

2. Tutors are motivated by student success. Consequently, as tutors observe their students gaining confidence in both the subject matter and in the area of being able to execute tasks independently, it becomes an intensely rewarding and satisfying experience for the tutor. Also, as the student becomes more disciplined, tutoring sessions become more efficient and tutors are able to apply themselves toward getting students confident and ahead of the curriculum. On the other hand, when students are disorganized, have no idea when tasks are due, and can't even find their homework, it's frustrating for everyone involved and the student doesn't get all they could out of the tutoring session.

3. Finally, parents can be confident that, if their student is effectively utilizing their Game Plan, then the tutoring sessions are being conducted in an efficient and effective manner, which maximizes the investment the parent has made in their child's education.

In the four years since I first met with the family who didn't want a math tutor in the house, I've learned a tremendous amount about executive functions and how deficits in this area can undermine the success of students, regardless of aptitude and natural intelligence. I've also been very proud and impressed with my tutors who embraced and pioneered the X-Skills Game Plan with enthusiasm and who always stay 100 percent focused on the student's success. Every day these talented "academic coaches" are changing the lives of students in tangible ways, as they help them sustain their performance at higher and higher levels. The excerpts below are just a few examples from tutor daily session reports (plus one from a student) of how powerful an impact they are making every day:

Tutors:

Steve has now gotten in the habit of checking his own PowerSchool to see his grades. I'm so glad! He's really taking initiative. He has stayed on top of his homework and writing it in his X-Skills notebook. He also schedules time to do his work and study ... He is doing such a great job and keeping up with his homework, studying, and keeping organized ... He has due dates set in mind and writes them in his X-Skills Game Plan. I am just so proud of him.

Amber and I worked today on a review of her X-Skills organizer, as she goes into the New Year holidays and then the debate tournament trip ... We talked about how she plans to prepare for this, and when she will be putting in time for extra preparations ... so we talked about some of the advantages and downsides of her current plans. Aside from the debate tournament, we looked at what she has scheduled for other classes, so that when January 6th rolls around, she isn't behind and unnecessarily in catch-up mode ... Amber is making great progress. She almost laughed at me tonight when I asked her if she was keeping track of anything electronically. She does EVERYTHING in her X-Skills organizer now and loves it!

Katie and I spent this session going over the X-Skills Game Plan. Since Katie started in the summer, the X-Skills Game Plan was not needed. However, now that school is in session the X-Skills Game Plan will be a great tool for Katie to use to help her with time management and organization ... In addition to her extracurricular activities, Katie already has quite a bit of homework. I could see that as Katie wrote down all of her homework and began blocking out time to complete it she started to realize that she has more homework to complete than she thought... so, the X-Skills Game Plan is going to be most useful for Katie in regards to time management.

Thirteen-year-old student:

At the beginning of the year, I was having problems understanding my teacher, and I was struggling in math. [My tutor] helped me understand my new subjects better. He also helped me with problems that did not make any sense to me. Before he started helping me, my grade was a 'C' and then when he started helping me, I got up to an 'A' almost immediately. [My tutor] also taught me many other skills like how to set up a schedule to complete and reach goals on big projects. This skill he taught me was very important this year because of all my big projects. This also helped me with the little things like turning in homework on time. In the end, I believe that ... because of him I brought my grade up and succeeded in math and I was able to make a comeback. Therefore, I believe that he was the best tutor for me and I would recommend him to others. So thanks, Dave, you did a lot to help me succeed.

4.2 Optimizing Brain Function
with Nutrition

By Kim Bjarnasson

Kim Bjarnasson's academic path has taken many turns. After completing her second Master's Degree she was accepted into the PhD program in Sociology at the University of Alberta. After completing her coursework and before embarking upon her research she took time off to have a baby. The birth of her daughter changed everything, including her academic focus. Having always appreciated the importance of a healthy lifestyle, Kim began researching the role of nutrition in healthy pregnancies and happy babies.

What she learned fueled her drive to learn more. Instead of completing her post-graduate degree Kim applied to the Nanaimo chapter of the Canadian School of Natural Nutrition where she graduated with honors. Her passion for the subject was evident, and upon graduation, she was asked to join the administrative team and now teaches courses that focus on the importance of optimum nutrition for the mind.

There are many factors that come into play to create the ideal conditions for academic success—knowing how to set a goal and devising a plan to achieve it, constructing the right mindset to envision yourself succeeding, and creating the right environment for learning, to name just a few. But all of these will be compromised unless/until we provide our body and brain with the fuel it needs to function optimally. There is no magic bullet, no single solution that will work for everyone; we are all different, unique in our biochemistry, lifestyles, circumstances, and hence, our needs. And thank goodness for that! For this reason, a holistic and integrated approach can provide a solid foundation upon which to nourish our body, mind, and soul, and in turn build academic success. So what exactly does this look like? Well, it consists of getting adequate exercise, sleep, and sustenance, and minimizing stress, fatigue, and nutritionally anemic food.[41]

While each of these aspects merits equal attention, the primary focus of this chapter will be on the role of nutrition—how what we eat influences how we think, and for that matter, who we are. And it really does, no question— *food is the external internalized.*[42] Food has the power to affect how we feel, think, and respond to stimuli in our environment.

According to the *Dietary Guidelines for Americans 2010*,[1] the top three sources of calories for individuals aged 2–18 are grain-based desserts,[2] pizza, and soda/energy/sports drinks. For the 14–18- year-old demographic, the number one source of calories is soda/energy/sports drinks, with boys consuming more of these added sugar calories than girls. Approximately 70 percent consume sugared beverages every day versus 60 percent of girls in the same age demographic.[43]

The U.S. *National Health and Nutrition Examination Survey* (NHANES) identifies the leading sources of added sugars in the U.S. population for people over two years of age as: sodas – 35.7%; grain-based desserts – 12.9%; fruit drinks – 10.5%; dairy desserts – 6.5%; candy – 6.1%; ready-to-eat cereals – 3.8%; sugars and honey – 3.5%; tea – 3.5%; breads – 2.1%; all other food categories[3] – 15.4%.[44] As we can see, soda is by far the leader. North Americans currently consume more liquid calories than at any time in history.[3]

Sadly, the bad news doesn't end here. The problem of poor nutrition and cognitive outcomes reaches beyond North America to anywhere the Standard American Diet (SAD) has been adopted. Research conducted in Perth, Australia, confirmed that eating a nutrient deficient diet, (particularly during important developmental periods such as adolescence) has long-term consequences. Taking advantage of a longitudinal study already under way, the researchers were able to

---

1   This document is published by the *US Department of Agriculture* in conjunction with the *US Department of Health and Human Services* (http://health.gov/dietaryguidelines/dga2010/DietaryGuidelines2010.pdf). Every year the U.S. Government, through the *Centers for Disease Control and Prevention*, surveys the American public on issues concerning their diet and lifestyle. The survey title is the *National Health and Nutrition Examination Survey*, and its data and reports are available online at http://www.cdc.gov/nchs/nhanes.htm.

2   Grain-based desserts include muffins, donuts, pastries, granola bars, cookies, etc.

3   Just an aside — the *"All other food categories"* category consists of many hidden sources of high fructose corn syrup (HFCS) including condiments and sauces like ketchup, BBQ sauce, spaghetti sauce, yogurt, and peanut butter.

review dietary data for approximately three thousand children from birth through adulthood (18 years). They found marked differences between teens consuming a *"Western-style diet"* (otherwise known as the SAD) characterized by high intakes of "takeaway food ... processed meat, soft drink(s), fried and refined food ... fried potato, crisps and red meat" and those consuming a *"healthy diet"* consisting of a high intake of whole grains, legumes, fish, fruit, and leafy greens. Adolescents eating the healthy diet scored significantly higher on cognitive performance tests, in math, reading comprehension and writing.[45] The bottom line: The *Standard American Diet* is simply not supportive of healthy brain function no matter where it's consumed.[46]

Some General Guidelines

Eating well—whether it's to promote brain function or just general overall health—can be pretty complicated. No carb, low carb, Mediterranean, paleo; it seems as though every day there is a new diet fad claiming miraculous benefits. But there is a way to simplify things. While these may not be hard and fast rules, if you can stick to the guidelines below, you're off to a good start:

Eat the rainbow—consume as many colors as you can from whole non-GMO organic fruits and vegetables;

Limit the refined whites—white salt, sugar, and flour, and replace them with whole grains and brown varieties, and if necessary, a little at a time;

Limit the amount of processed foods you eat, particularly those with more than five ingredients, or ingredients you've never heard of;

Reduce consumption of pop, energy drinks and fruit juice in your diet, reserving them for special occasions (or remove them completely) and replacing them with water and whole fruits and vegetables;

Try to replace industrially raised and produced animal products with grass fed organic varieties;

Replace refined vegetable oils such as sunflower, safflower, corn and canola with butter, coconut oil and olive oils to reduce contact with GMO crops.

Employ the 80/20 rule, which means if you're doing right by your body 80 percent of the time, the remaining 20 percent won't even register. So don't deny yourself your favorite treats, just reserve them for occasional use. Food is one of life's pleasures, don't miss out on it!

As you may be aware, there are a lot of additives, preservatives, and other chemicals being put into our foods. And let's be honest, do we really know exactly what they're doing to us? Let's dig a little deeper and find out why it's important to know what's going into our food and our bodies.

The Fructose — Glucose Effect

While consumption of refined carbohydrates is approaching 50 percent of our daily calories, research over the last five years is making it increasingly clear that it's the calories from sugar-sweetened beverages that are so detrimental to our physical and mental health.[47] Unobstructed by fiber, fat, and protein (not to mention devoid of vitamins, minerals and antioxidants), acute sucrose consumption (of which sugar-sweetened beverages apply) sees sucrose enter the bloodstream quickly, flooding the body with glucose and the liver with fructose. And what happens next? Let's take a look...

GLUCOSE

Acute concentrations of glucose, again, as found in a can of pop or juice box, triggers a cyclic rise and fall in blood sugar levels, and with it an emotional and metabolic roller coaster that makes any effort at focus and concentration a serious challenge. And while glucose is necessary to immune function, defending our body from foreign invaders is an energy intensive process. However, excessive acute glucose ingestion (again, equivalent to a can of soda or a juice box)[4] depresses the immune system for up to five hours, reducing the body's resistance to infection.[5,48]

Sugar also disrupts our body's natural pH (7.4) making it more acidic, throwing off oxygen delivery to cells, turning formerly constructive enzymes destructive, and disrupting mineral absorption and balance.[49] In order to return our blood to its optimal pH, we need to remove excess sugar from our diet, consume a variety of alkaline foods, including green vegetables, cauliflower, beets, apples, avocados, and almonds, and drink more water.[50]

And finally, if all this weren't bad enough, sugar establishes cravings not unlike other well-known substances of abuse including cocaine, heroin, and alcohol. Research conducted in the last five years has identified the dopamine reward pathways on which sugar travels, and they are similar to those traveled by cocaine, triggering reinforcement and habituation of the said substance. Would this not explain why we can be satisfied with one serving (or maybe two) of our favorite vegetable but have trouble resisting seconds and

---

4   Crazy fact: 12oz of apple juice has the SAME amount of sugar as 12oz of coke. Seriously, look it up! And a little kitchen trick to help you visualize how much sugar we're talking about: 4 grams = 1 tsp

5   Individuals with diabetes mellitus tend towards impaired neutrophilic phagocytosis as compared to normal subjects, which suggests that high blood glucose and insulin resistance lend themselves to depressed immune function and susceptibility to infection (Sanchez et al., 1973).

thirds of our favorite dessert, sometimes finding it necessary to enlist some pretty extreme willpower measures?[51] Sugar essentially tricks our brain into thinking we want more, and more, and more, by over-riding our satiation pathways and keeping us craving that next sweet hit.[52]

FRUCTOSE

Fructose, on the other hand, cannot be used as energy by our organs and tissues like glucose can, but for one—the liver. In the liver, fructose is metabolized into triglycerides (fat), free fatty acids and uric acid, contributing to high blood pressure, obesity, insulin resistance, hyperglycemia and fatty liver disease—otherwise known as *metabolic syndrome.*[6,53] And because fructose doesn't trigger insulin release like glucose, our natural satiety cycle doesn't get initiated.[54] Without the concomitant dance of insulin and leptin, our brain does not receive the message that our stomach is full and that we should stop eating. What does this mean? Well, we think we're still hungry even though we've satisfied our body's need for food.[7] So even

---

6   For those interested in the biochemistry of fructose metabolism check out the diagram and content at www.nofructose.com/introduction/metabolism/.

7   During glucose metabolism, insulin is released into the bloodstream, which shuttles glucose into all the cells of our body where, depending upon the organ and its function, it is broken down into ATP, glycogen, and triglycerides (fat), in that order. Glucose is converted to fat only when the other two options are maximized. When the triglycerides reach adipose tissue, leptin (the "I'm full" hormone), which is secreted from fat cells, is released to instruct the hypothalamus to stop eating. At the same time, ghrelin (the "I'm hungry" hormone), which is released from cells in the stomach lining when our stomachs are empty, travelling to the hypothalamus to get us foraging for food, is suppressed when the stomach lining is stretched, as when we're full. However, for reasons not entirely clear, fructose interferes with this process, so the brain continues to receive the *'I'm hungry'* message, and never gets the one telling it *'I'm full'*, so we continue to eat, and all the extra calories are stored as fat (Lustig, 2009; Teff, 2013).

though high concentrations of glucose and fructose are metabolized differently, the result is the same—a tendency to overeat, and of mostly refined carbohydrate-rich foods.[55]

What about Artificial Sweeteners?

So if it's sugar from sweetened beverages that's the problem, why not just consume the type sweetened with artificial sweeteners? I mean, if a single can of coke contains 10 tsp. of sugar, alone exceeding the recommended daily allowance of between 7–9 tsp. of added sugar,[8] why not just go with the calorie-free versions? Current research has found that artificial sweeteners such as sucralose, saccharin, and aspartame create a blood-sugar spike greater than that of glucose due to alterations in intestinal microbiota upon consumption, as well as the development of glucose intolerance, dysbiosis and with regular use, metabolic syndrome.[56]

Aspartame, the most commonly used artificial sweetener on the market, has also been linked to neurological problems such as migraines, dizziness, seizures, numbness, vision problems, memory loss, muscle spasms, tachycardia, tinnitus, apoptosis (programmed cell death), and the list goes on and on. The Environmental Protection Agency (EPA) has even listed aspartame in its database of developmental neurotoxicants under the category *Chemicals with Substantial Evidence of Developmental Toxicity.*[9] It's that bad.

Aspartame is a chemical excitotoxin, a *neurotoxin*, which means it is poisonous to nerve tissue and stimulates neurons to fire repeatedly until they die. Its chemical structure is phenylalanine, aspartic acid, and methanol. The first two ingredients (phenylalanine and aspartic

---

8   Added sugars do not include the natural sugar found in fruit or other carbohydrate foods such as whole grains, legumes, and beans.

9   See for yourself: http://www.epa.gov/ncct/toxcast/files/summit/48P%20 Mundy%20TDAS.pdf

acid) are naturally occurring amino acids necessary for proper neurological functioning. However, their concentrations in the aspartame molecule are in much greater quantities than what would occur naturally in the diet, causing excessive neuronal activity. The third ingredient, methanol, or wood alcohol, is metabolized into formaldehyde in the body creating systemic toxicity, oxidative stress, and cellular damage/death due to excessive free radical production.[57] Aspartame is a poison, and no one denies it, and the more you consume, the worse the neurological effects. Fortunately, there's an upside to this story. In spite of all the damage inflicted on the nervous system by this toxic chemical, when aspartame is removed from the diet, the symptoms largely disappear; the brain is that resilient.[10]

A Brief Lesson in Brain Development

The brain, unlike other organs in the body, isn't functionally mature until our mid-twenties, and its development is not a straightforward cohesive process. Different parts of the brain expand at different times. For instance, the temporal and parietal lobes, responsible for processing sensory information and language among other functions, develop before the frontal lobe, where consciousness, critical thinking and higher thought processes occur. And in adolescence, it's the *pre*frontal cortex (responsible for abstract thought, reasoning, self-regulation, and problem solving) and hippocampus (memory and learning) specifically that undergo major fine-tuning, reinforcing neuronal connections that are strong, and pruning back those that are weak, to create efficient and effective neurological networks. But even here we see variations in timelines—neurological systems responsible for logical reasoning mature around the age of 16, while those involved in self-regulation and self-control come together between ages 18–20.[58] So this can be a very complicated

---

10   For an insightful look into one woman's journey with aspartame check out the documentary "Sweet Misery: A Poisoned World."

time for teens and parents, requiring a great deal of patience and understanding, and a good supply of micro and macronutrients to make these growth periods as smooth and stable as possible.

Given the current state of the North American population, it's no surprise that the relationship between nutrition and cognition is a hot topic these days. Advances in neuroscience and brain-scan imaging have allowed us to key in on those parts of the brain most active while we learn a new task, process information, and retrieve a memory. We can now see, in *real time,* our brains at work. Simply amazing! But while we hear the term cognition repeated over and over in these conversations, we don't often receive a definition. What does cognitive function really mean? We know we want it to be optimal, but what exactly are we trying to optimize? Well, human cognition falls into six basic areas: executive functioning,[11] memory, attention, perception and psychomotor and language skills.[59] These are what we want to maximize for optimal cognitive function.

What We Need

The human brain has been an endless source of fascination for as long as we've known it exists, with the Greeks making great strides in mapping its anatomical structure, documenting with great care every "knob, protrusion, canal and crease" long before their functions were known. Naming these structures, therefore, was a creative and decorative act, seeing fantastical names such as the *zonules of Zinn,* the *tract of Goll,* the *field of Forel* and *area 23 of Hippo,* ascribed to what could otherwise be described as somewhat slimy and squishy bulges of gray matter, much like the consistency of tofu.[60]

---

11   Executive function is an umbrella term for "the management of cognitive processes, including working memory, reasoning, task flexibility, and problem solving as well as planning and execution." (https://en.wikipedia.org/wiki/Executive_functions)

Fortunately, the last hundred years has brought with it great strides in our physiological understanding of the brain, giving texture to these terms, and shedding light on how remarkably intricate and complex that gray matter is. But like any intricate structure made up of a dizzying number of microscopic components, the more we can see, the more questions we have. And while this does mean there is always more to learn, we have amassed a considerable body of knowledge, and with it, cultivated a firm grounding of some basic mechanical physiology. Here are some fun well-known neurological facts:

- We have over 100 billion neurons in our brain, making over 100 trillion connections between them; this is roughly equivalent to the number of trees in the Amazon rain forest (if they weren't being removed by acres per day), and the connection that would be made between each leaf on each of its branches.

- Our brain is composed of over 60 percent fat.

- An adult brain accounts for two percent of our body mass but uses 25 percent of our supply of oxygen and glucose; a baby's brain uses 50 percent of its glucose.

- Lack of oxygen to the brain for more than five minutes will result in permanent brain damage.

- New brain connections are made every time we form a new memory or have a thought, and we have over 700,000 thoughts every day.

- Half of our genes transcribe for the complex design of our brain.

The right combination of macronutrients (protein, fats, and complex carbohydrates) and micronutrients (vitamins and minerals) is essential to the growth and maturation of the brain, including building and maintaining the structure and function of brain tissue and ensuring healthy neurochemistry and cellular communication.[61] But before we dive into the realm of nutrition, let's take a few minutes and talk about a couple of the other important ingredients for optimal cognitive function and academic success—stress management and exercise.[62]

Stress

There is no shortage of research on the relationship between cognitive function and stress.[63] Chronic stress, whether it be due to busy schedules, emotional difficulties, lack of sleep or poor nutrition (Sound familiar? Even a little?), will cause cellular changes in parts of the brain (the hippocampus, frontal cortex, and hypothalamus)[64] responsible for focused attention, perception, short-term memory, and learning.[65]

Cortisol and adrenalin are hormones that are released into the bloodstream during times of stress, triggering a physiological cascade that shuts some body systems down (digestive, immune, and reproductive, for instance) in order to elevate the activity of others (muscular-skeletal, cardiovascular, and nervous). This vital automatic reaction to a real or perceived threat (stressor) is known as the *stress response* and is initiated by the attendant activation of the sympathetic nervous system and hypothalamic-pituitary-adrenal (HPA) axis. The stress response allows us to concentrate our energy resources in certain organ systems in times of emergency, and when we've survived the attack, terminate, so as to allow a smooth physiological transition back to homeostasis with the help of the parasympathetic nervous system. These two systems have a synergistic relationship, and when under conditions of acute stress, it works and does so seamlessly.

However, many people spend much of their day under conditions of chronic stress—*"running on adrenalin,"* which means operating without the full function of all body systems. Considering just two of these organ systems, when we are in full sympathetic mode, we are concentrating our body's energy, it's ATP, in those parts of the body designed to get us somewhere (our muscles and our CV system; think *fight or flight*) and shutting down those designed to fuel and protect the body (the digestive and immune systems—think *rest and digest*). What does this mean? Well, for one, it means that we're eating without proper digestion. Food can't be broken down into its component parts, so the finer elements of that food, the micro- and macro-nutrients can't circulate through the body to feed the cells. What does enter the bloodstream are food particles too large for the body to recognize, foreign substances that the immune system would normally take care of, but with it being shut down, are free to circulate, causing havoc to the body and brain; a condition known as stress-induced immunosuppression.[66] The result: poor nutrient absorption, increased inflammation, and hence, poor cellular function; the brain isn't getting what it needs for optimal development and processing.

Second, chronic elevated cortisol levels also suppress memory formation, and hence, learning, as cortisol causes the neuron extensions in the hippocampus to shrivel, preventing adequate neural communication so that the neurons can't talk to each other. Fortunately, the damage caused to these neurons isn't permanent. Breaking the stress cycle and reducing chronically circulating cortisol allows the neurons to heal and grow back, reopening those channels of communication.[67] Regular exercise, yoga, tai chi, or some form of meditative practice, are well-documented means of reversing the stress response and inducing the relaxation response. Meditative practices such as yoga are focused on quieting the mind, focusing the breath, and bringing equilibrium back to the body by eliciting the parasympathetic nervous system (remember "rest and digest?")[68]. It's during these times of calm that our body rebuilds, repairs and cleanses.[69] And really, finding a quiet minute to listen to your favorite music will do this too! Whatever you find relaxing.

Exercise

John Ratey, in his best-selling book *Spark*, enthusiastically shares a conversation he has with a physical education teacher/football coach from Naperville Central High School in Illinois, Paul Zientarski.[70] Zientarski implemented a fitness regime for all his students that consisted of between 30 minutes and one hour of aerobic activity five days a week. It didn't take long for his experiment to produce measurable results, showing marked improvements in his students' academic performance and attitudes toward school, and a welcome increase in self-confidence that accompanied their individual successes. Ratey sees Naperville as a powerful case study of how aerobic activity can transform our bodies and minds. As coach Zientarski states, his department creates the brain cells, while it's up to the teachers to fill them.

Research is clear on this point: aerobic exercise strengthens neural plasticity.[71] By stimulating the production of brain-derived neurotrophic factor (BDNF), a protein that supports the maintenance and survival of existing neurons, exercise strengthens the communication links between them, particularly in those areas of the brain focused on learning, memory, and higher thinking.[72]

While this is evidence enough to awaken a personal commitment to get moving, exercising also serves as a catalyst for nutrient distribution, and that includes glucose. Exercise, especially of the aerobic variety, increases blood circulation, and it's via the blood that important vitamins and minerals are delivered to every cell in our body, including the brain. So, the greater the circulation of blood, the greater the distribution of nutrients.[73] Some researchers actually go so far as to suggest that, as regards optimal cognitive function, the primary contribution that exercise makes is the delivery of nutrients.[74] Exercise is a serious win-win!

Okay, Here are the Goods on Nutrition: The Macronutrients — Carbohydrates, Fats and Protein

CARBOHYDRATES

All carbohydrates are members of the plant family—fruit, vegetables, grasses, legumes, and grains. However, as you may have gleaned from the discussion on sugar, while they are all a source of that life-giving nutrient—glucose—their metabolics of delivery are not the same. Generally speaking, carbohydrates come in two forms, simple and complex. Simple carbohydrates/sugars are those I spent considerable time on when discussing sugar. These are mono- and disaccharides (one and two chain sugars) that are very easily broken down and digested, and hence enter the circulation very quickly. Simple sugars are important sources of energy when needed immediately, but not so good over the long term. Sugar/sucrose and fruit consist of simple sugars.

Complex carbohydrates are polysaccharides (long chain sugars) and starches that provide a sustained and steady release of glucose. As complex carbohydrates are members of the plant family they tend to be rich in fiber and a range of vitamins and minerals, making them nutrient rich and slow to break down and digest. Dietary sources include whole grains, rice, legumes, oats, all vegetables, corn, potatoes, and sweet potatoes.

THE FATS

During the 1980s, the prevalence of cardiovascular disease was on the rise, and scientists were beginning to make the connection between dietary fat and heart disease. Saturated fats quickly rose to enemy status in the minds of Americans, with a hungry food industry salivating to sink its teeth into a solution. Surely, if the accumulation of arterial fat was the problem, the solution was as simple as cutting fat from the diet. The villains—saturated animal fats in the form of high-fat dairy products (butter, cheese, milk, yogurt), fatty cuts of meat, fatty fish, and eggs (once thought to be the perfect food!). The food industry rose to the challenge and grocery shelves quickly filled with an abundance of highly processed low-fat high-carb products.

Well, here we are, thirty-five years later, and the research is clear—heart disease is still a serious problem, but to it, has been added skyrocketing rates of Type 2 diabetes, obesity, and high blood pressure. A perfect pharmaceutical storm, otherwise known as "metabolic syndrome." The last five years has seen an increasing consensus in the scientific community: saturated fats were not the main contributor to heart disease, but rather trans-fats.[75] Turns out saturated fat may not have been the villain after all. The problem was its replacement with trans fats—hydrogenated vegetable oils in the form of margarine, and highly refined carbohydrates—the "refined whites" as I like to refer to them—something had to make the food taste good! With a decrease in fat and consequent increase in refined carbs, we were faced with a whole new set of physical and mental health problems necessitating treatment.

So, let's make friends with fat again! Here's the cast: *saturated and monounsaturated fats, polyunsaturated fats (Omega 3 & 6) and cholesterol*. The brain, as previously mentioned, consists of 60 percent fat, and as such, is reliant upon a few specific types of fat present in the right quantities and combinations. In other words, not too much, and not too little! All of these fats play important roles in creating a strong cellular membrane and ensuring smooth cellular function and communication.

SATURATED AND MONOUNSATURATED FATS

Saturated fats are those that remain solid at room temperature, so include butter, suet, coconut and palm oils, and foods high in saturated fats including cheese, cream, baking chocolate and red meat. These are the oils you want to fry with as they have a high-smoke point (which means they won't burn as easily at high temperatures and become carcinogenic). Again, saturated fats are important for cellular function and hormone production, so use them, but do so in moderation, and lean toward the plant-based varieties.

Monounsaturated fats are typically liquid at room temperature but will solidify when cold, and include olive oil, avocado oil, peanut and sesame oils, safflower, and canola oils, with food sources including nuts, seeds, olives, and avocados. These can be used more liberally than the saturated fats, particularly in their whole food forms. Monounsaturated oils should not be used for frying as they have a low smoke point and will begin to burn at high temperatures, but are great for baking and in dressings. Monounsaturated fats help reduce the bad cholesterol[12] (low-density lipoproteins transport cholesterol throughout the body) in our bodies and are important for cellular membrane structure.

POLYUNSATURATED FATTY ACIDS (PUFAS)

The PUFAs we're going to concentrate on are those categorized as *Essential Fatty Acids* (EFAs),[13] in particular, Omega 3 (alpha-linolenic acid or ALA) and Omega 6 (linoleic acid or LA). Omega 3 and Omega 6 work synergistically to improve bone health.

Optimally, we will see a balance at 1:1, but because of the increasing amount of Omega 6 in the diet due to high vegetable oil consumption

---

12 We have two types of cholesterol transporters: *low-density lipoproteins* (LDL) and *high-density lipoproteins* (HDL). Essentially, LDLs carry surplus cholesterol from animal products to various organs in the body via the blood stream. HDLs transport cholesterol to the liver.

13 Essential fatty acids are PUFAs that cannot be synthesized by the body from other sources of dietary fat so they must come from the diet.

and lower fish intake, the balance has shifted to something in the realm of 20:1 (Omega 6 to Omega 3). When the balance is this skewed, Omega 6 can interfere with the positive anti-inflammatory work done by Omega 3 shifting the physiological status of the tissues toward an inflammatory state, creating an environment ripe for infection and disease. It's important, therefore, to get that ratio as close to 1:1 as possible.[76]

Omega 3

Omega 3 is important for neural communication and supports the production of BDNF (brain-derived neurotrophic factor), which stimulates cellular mechanisms central to learning and memory. Omega 3 also reduces inflammation in the brain and body, stabilizes mood, and reduces incidences of depression and anxiety, among a number of other physiological and neurological functions. Food sources of Omega 3 include cold-water fatty fish (krill, herring, sardines, tuna, and salmon), flax, hemp, pumpkin seeds, and walnuts, as well as their associated oils. As a supplement, between 500–1000 mg of a good quality fish oil free of contaminants daily will do the trick.

Omega 3 can also be converted to two other essential fatty acids, eicosapentaenoic acid (EPA) and docosahexaenoic acid (DHA), each serving important neurological and physiological functions.[14] While EPA is a relatively easy synthesis from Omega 3, DHA is not, and so requires a pre-synthesized dietary source. This can include a good quality fish oil, or for those on a vegetarian or vegan diet, an algae supplement available at your local health food store. And if you're

---

14   DHA is particularly protective against cognitive decline associated with dementia and Alzheimer's disease, so best to ensure adequate intake now so as to maintain good cognitive function for as long as possible! For a particularly good list of academic articles on the role of Omega 3, EPA and DHA in the diet see the University of Maryland Medical Center's *Overview of Omega-3 fatty acids* reference list (http://umm.edu/health/medical/altmed/supplement/omega3-fatty-acids).

already taking an Omega 3 fish oil supplement, there's no need to add another here, as fish oil is rich in EPA and DHA.

Omega 6

Like Omega 3, Omega 6 plays an important role in optimal neurological function and cellular communication. It also reduces incidences and symptoms of ADHD, supports overall physical growth and development, and is a natural treatment for skin disorders such as eczema and dermatitis. Dietary sources include eggs, avocados, coconut, pumpkin seeds, cashews, pecans and walnuts and vegetable oils such as sunflower, safflower, soy, sesame, and corn. Supplemental forms include Evening Primrose Oil (EPO) and spirulina blue-green algae.

CHOLESTEROL

Cholesterol is essential to life, vital to proper cellular function, synthesis of vitamin D and bile acids, and hormone production. In fact, without adequate cholesterol, our bodies couldn't make the hormones essential for reproduction and the stress response. Like the other fats, every cell in the body requires cholesterol, but unlike the others, with a balanced diet including the good healthy fats listed above, our body can produce all the cholesterol we need.[15]

PROTEIN

Protein is the building block of life, providing the necessary raw materials in the form of *amino acids* for the construction of our body's muscles, organs, and tissues, and that includes the brain

---

15　The chemical structure of cholesterol is slightly different from the other types of fat we've talked about, consisting of a sterol (steroid derivative) lipid molecule. While all cells of the body synthesize cholesterol, the main manufacturing center is the liver, with the intestines, adrenal glands and reproductive organs producing some as well.

(protein makes up much of the remaining 40 percent after fat). Amino acids also form the chemicals that allow our various organs, including and most importantly, the brain, to communicate with one another—these being our neurotransmitters and a number of our hormones. Without an adequate supply of essential amino acids neurological function will be compromised, leading to problems with concentration, comprehension, attention, focus, learning and memory, not to mention mood and neurological disorders such as depression, anxiety, ADHD, and bipolar disorder. Not the best conditions for optimal student success.

There is a total of 20 amino acids, 10 of which are essential, meaning that we must get them from our diet,[16] with the remaining 10 synthesized from among the essential 10. While all foods contain some amount of these essential amino acids, the concentrations vary. While virtually all animal sources contain sufficient quantities of the essential amino acids (considered "complete proteins") many plant sources do not, sometimes proving deficient in one or more of these essential amino acids. However, with careful attention to proper food combining principles, someone following a vegetarian or vegan diet should be able to acquire all of the necessary essential amino acids.

While food sources of amino acids are plentiful, whether they be animal or plant based, what's important is to ensure that they are fresh and of good quality, and whenever possible, organic. For animal products this means that the animals eat as natural a diet

---

16 The nine essential amino acids are tryptophan, threonine, isoleucine, leucine, lysine, methionine, phenylalanine, valine, and histidine. The remaining 11 can be synthesized from these. And these numbers aren't firm. As you'll notice if you do a bit of research, some sources will quote a total of 23 amino acids, eight, or sometimes ten, of which are essential. When it comes to the human body we're literally learning something new every day, so while the number or balance of amino acids may change, the facts of their importance to optimal brain function don't. We need protein in our diet, and if we're consuming adequate amounts, whether in complete form or via food combining, our body and brain will be fueled for success.

as possible, limiting the amount of time they are fed a grain-based diet and are free of hormones and antibiotics. For plants, we want to see that they are non-GMO and free of chemical pesticides and herbicides. So here's the list!

Animal sources of complete proteins include the following:

- Meat, fish, poultry, eggs, dairy products...done!

Plant sources of complete proteins:

- Quinoa, buckwheat, amaranth, hempseed, chia, soy, nutritional yeast, and spirulina.

If you don't feel confident that you're consuming enough complete plant-based proteins, not to worry. By following the simple principles of food combining you'll ensure your body receives an adequate supply of all nine essential amino acids. And you don't have to eat the foods together as a meal, but just at some point during your day. Your body will do the rest.

One rule of food combining is to consume legumes and Poaceae[17] or grains within a 24-hour period. Common legumes include lentils, soybeans, chickpeas, beans (such as runner, fava, broad, lima, kidney, black, pinto), peas, clover, and alfalfa.

Food combining has been common practice for centuries, with many traditional ethnic combinations remaining staples in many households. Some of these include Mexican beans and corn, Japanese soybeans and rice, Cajun red beans and rice, or Indian dal and rice or roti. All of these meals combine legumes with grass grains to provide a meal that is rich in all essential amino acids.

---

17   Poaceae, also known as grasses, are of the flowering plant family. Those included under its title provide food to the world's populations. Common Poaceae include corn, wheat, rice, barley, and millet.

The Micronutrients—Vitamins, Minerals and Phytonutrients

VITAMINS AND MINERALS

Micronutrients, our vitamins, and minerals, are integral to optimal neurological function, and health. Through a cellular mechanism called *methylation*, a series of reactions occur continuously in every cell in the body, providing our brains with the nutrients they need to maintain and fuel optimal cellular communication, as well as the tools they need to remain free of toxic overload.

Through the environment, and that means everything we eat, the air we breathe, the water we drink, how we deal with stress and how much sleep and exercise we get, toxins make their way past our major biological lines of defense (the intestinal wall, our immune system, and the blood brain barrier) and pollute our brain. Chemical pesticides and herbicides, artificial colors and flavors, air pollutants, excess cortisol, all compromise our brain's ability to function properly. But if our methylation cycle is running optimally and we're getting adequate supplies of the amino acids, vitamins, and minerals listed above, we can synthesize our own antioxidant and heavy metal chelator—commonly known as Glutathione and Metallothionein. These are our body's own workhorses. Living toxin free is difficult within the context of modern life, but with optimal nutrition through a whole foods diet, we can act preventatively to stave off much of the potential damage caused by toxic overload.

To list the known range of benefits from every vitamin and mineral that plays a role in optimal neurological function is impossible within the confines of this chapter. What I've included are those that are of critical importance to optimal brain function. So here's what we need:

The Family of B Vitamins

When considering cognitive function, there is no category of vitamins that play a larger role than that of the B vitamin family. Of the B vitamins, the lead actors are vitamins B12 (cobalamin), B9 (folate), B6 (pyridoxine) and B3 (niacin). Food sources include the following:

> B12—red meat, fish, eggs, dairy products, nutritional yeast[18]
>
> B9—organ meats, legumes (beans, chickpeas, lentils), sunflower seeds, edamame (fresh soy beans), avocado, papaya, leafy greens, broccoli, asparagus
>
> B6—red meat, pork, fish, poultry, organ meats, whole grains, wheat bran, oatmeal, soy (tempeh, tofu, miso), nuts, lentils, potatoes/sweet potatoes with skin, carrots, bananas, avocado
>
> B3—liver, red meat, pork, poultry, fish, soy (tempeh, miso, tofu), eggs, dairy products, mushrooms, cashews, almonds, sunflower seeds, legumes, oatmeal, wheat bran/germ, bran cereals, marmite, or vegemite.

If you don't feel confident that you are getting adequate amounts of B vitamins from your diet, a good quality B-Complex vitamin from your local health food store can provide peace of mind. And as the family of B vitamins is water soluble, you'll simply excrete that which you don't need.

---

18 People following a vegetarian or vegan diet may have trouble getting enough B12 from their diet alone so may want to supplement. The most bioavailable form of B12 is called *methylcobalamin*, a sub-lingual form that is available at your local health food store.

Vitamin C

Important in the methylation pathway, and helps maintain immune function.

This one is easy—food sources include virtually all bright colored fruits and vegetables (reds, yellows, oranges, greens). Done!

Vitamin D

Biosynthesized via cholesterol, vitamin D helps to reduce inflammation in the brain and can be effective at staving off Seasonal Affective Disorder (SAD) during the short days of winter. Vitamin D is a fat-soluble vitamin so requires fat to make it bio-available. It can also be stored in the body.

Because it was felt people generally were deficient in vitamin D, many dairy products and dairy substitutes such as rice, almond, and soy beverages have been fortified with vitamin D. However, good whole food sources include fish and fish oils, pork, and eggs.

Calcium

Calcium is important for cellular communication and in the methylation pathway.

While dairy foods have been touted as *THE* source of calcium in a healthy diet, opinions are starting to change with plant-based sources of calcium becoming increasingly popular. So, some non-dairy sources include collard greens, spinach, kale, turnip and turnip greens, tofu (in all its forms), blackstrap molasses and fish (particularly sardines and salmon).

Magnesium

Magnesium is involved in over 300 reactions in the body, many to do with regulating mood, sleep cycles, muscular function, and the methylation pathway.

Food sources are plentiful and include dark leafy greens, nuts, seeds, fish, legumes, whole grains, avocados, bananas, dried fruit, and dark chocolate.

Zinc

Zinc is the most commonly deficient nutrient in the body, yet crucial for mental health, particularly as it concerns memory storage and retrieval, attention, concentration, immune function, and again, in the methylation pathways. Fortunately, a little goes a long way, and given that it isn't the easiest sourced mineral, many processed foods are fortified with zinc.

Food sources include oysters, organ meats, fish, pork, dairy products, pumpkin seeds, baked beans, fermented soy products such as tempeh and miso and wheat germ.

Sulfur

Sulfur is an important cofactor in the methylation pathway and the synthesis of our antioxidant and heavy metal chelator—those workhorses I spoke of earlier— Glutathione and Metallothionein. So getting a steady supply from our diet is important, but fortunately pretty easy.

Sulfur-rich foods include cruciferous vegetables such as broccoli, cauliflower, kale, cabbage and Brussel sprouts, garlic, onions, eggs, fish, red meat, poultry, nuts, and legumes. See! Easy.

A final note on minerals. Himalayan pink salt and gray sea salt are rich in many of the minerals our bodies need for optimal function, and are naturally present in the right concentrations. Minerals work synergistically, and an imbalance in one can throw off the availability of others, which is part of the problem with what has come to be our staple salt—NaCl, sodium chloride. This combination isn't terrible in itself, but with liberal use can disrupt our body's mineral equilibrium, and lead to problems with high blood pressure and fluid balance. Pink and gray salt can and should replace white table salt, and believe me, once you've tried a natural salt you'll never go back, and will reap the positive health benefits.

Phytonutrients

Phytonutrients, also referred to as phytochemicals, is an umbrella term for the biologically active compounds derived from the plant family—fruits, vegetables, legumes, grains, and grasses. While scientists have identified over two thousand phytochemicals to date, there are suspected to be upwards of four thousand phytochemicals among the plant family. Some common nutrients include phytosterols, antioxidants, carotenoids, polyphenols, resveratrol, isoflavones, and flavonoids. The health benefits phytonutrients provide are many, including assisting the body in the elimination of free radicals, helping reduce inflammation, supporting neural plasticity and the strengthening connections between neurons which, as we know by now, is the basis of learning, memory formation, and memory retrieval.

Dietary sources of some common phytonutrients include the following:[19]

> *Phytosterols*—green leafy vegetables, cucumbers, beet greens, seeds, nuts and capers

> *Antioxidants*—grapes, blue/red berries, nuts, dark green vegetables, orange and red vegetables, sweet potatoes, and tea

---

19　For an extensive list of phytonutrients and their health giving properties, I suggest the following website: *Linus Pauling Institute*: http://lpi.oregonstate.edu/infocenter/phytochemicals

Carotenoids—orange-colored fruit and vegetables including sweet potatoes, carrots, squash, peppers, cantaloupe, apricots, dark leafy greens, broccoli, and peas

Polyphenols—spices (most especially, curcumin), herbs, cocoa powder, dark chocolate, flaxseed, nuts, and elderberry

Resveratrol—red and purple grapes, blueberries, and dark chocolate

Isoflavones—soy is the major sources of isoflavones in all its forms (edamame, tempeh, miso, tofu)

Flavonoids—all berries, brightly colored fruits and vegetables, spices, nuts, and beans

Summary

So here we are, on our way to academic success, and all it took was a little reminder of how important *real food is*. You know, the kind that doesn't come with a list of ingredients, or if it does, it's less than five? Seriously, creating the optimal biological environment for success isn't hard, it just takes a little redirection. The food industry has tried to convince us that it can provide everything our body and brain need better than nature can. But slowly we're seeing that the only thing it can effectively provide is convenience, and sometimes that's even an illusion.

5. The Power of Standing Out

5.1 How to Help Your Child Stand Out

By Jon-Anthony Lui

Jon-Anthony Lui came from an entrepreneurial family—his father was a successful businessman and worked in franchising. Jon-Anthony found his niche—and his passion—when he joined the Tutor Doctor family. At Tutor Doctor, Jon-Anthony navigates his business through uncharted waters. His vision is to help students, families, tutors, team members, and fellow franchisees achieve their goals and see the positive possibilities. He cares about developing people (himself included), processes, and systems in order to turn barriers into breakthroughs and set new records.

Remember those popular kids at school? The ones the teachers loved and the students worshiped? What did they have that others didn't? They weren't always the best looking or most athletic students and they certainly weren't always the smartest. But those magical students who stood out from the crowd really did benefit: students loved them, teachers spent more time with them, and they got more opportunities than the rest of the class.

Outstanding students get more positive reinforcement and a better academic experience, meaning that they have a healthier attitude to learning. All of these factors improve their confidence and any teacher or tutor will tell you that when it comes to academic success, confidence is key.

Showing Appreciation for Learning

Teaching children to think of others first will enable them to stand out in a crowd. This doesn't need to come at the expense of winning, but consideration is an invaluable personality trait for them to acquire. Showing consideration to their classmates and expressing their appreciation for their teacher is a wonderful way to be exceptional. This has been the stalwart of teacher's pets throughout the ages; just think of leaving an apple on the teacher's desk—a small act of consideration that goes a long way.

Consideration at home will help them to get along with their siblings and with you. One way to instill consideration is to ask them to do one kind thing each day. This can be as simple as thanking a teacher for all their hard work or as demanding as volunteering at a local charity.

Showing gratitude and appreciation to teachers should be genuine; insincere gestures can actually work against them.

Set Goals and Make them Known

Would you set out for a hike in the woods without a map or compass? Ever noticed that when you set goals for each day, you become super-efficient at getting things done? Well, your child's academic career is exactly the same: without direction they simply won't know where they are going. They won't know just how much effort to put in either.

Get them to set their own goals like; "I want to be an honor roll student." Now we're going somewhere! When they have goals, they have direction and they know where they are headed. They also know how much work they have to put in if they want to reach their goals.

Before we get ahead of ourselves, speak with teachers and tutors to determine your child's strengths and weaknesses. The goals they set should be realistic and there should be both short and long-term goals that guide them every step of the way. Goal setting should be collaborative; getting your child to set their own goals will ensure participation—we all know how children respond to being told what to do!

A recent study by Dominican University showed that people were more likely to reach goals if they shared them. People who kept their goals to themselves only achieved success around 35 percent of the time, while those who wrote them down and enlisted the help of others, achieved their goals 70 percent of the time.[77]

Once your child has set their long and short-term goals, they should write them down in a prominent place. Make posters for their rooms or a cover for their homework book. If they are visual learners, get them to draw pictures of their goals for the year.

They should then share their goals with their teachers and ask for help in achieving them. The study also showed that regular progress reports were instrumental to success, so a monthly check-in with teachers to ask how they are doing will help students to gauge their progress and pick up the pace where they need to. It will also show the teacher that they are engaged, that they care and the teacher is far more likely to give them the attention they need to reach those goals.

Teachers often feel unappreciated; hearing your child ask for help and thank them for their input helps to inspire them too.

Using the Summer to Get Ahead

Sometimes being the popular kid means doing things that aren't popular. One of these is summer learning. Research shows that kids lose about 30 percent of the reading and math gains they made over the previous year during the long summer vacation, with lower income children experiencing the greatest loss.[78]

Just a couple of hours a week of tutoring over the summer vacation can mean that your child not only maintains the academic progress they made over the last school year but also that they can move ahead of the class.

If your child is struggling, a little learning over the vacation will not only fill in the missing building blocks to their foundation of knowledge, it can also instill the executive skills they need to be successful, independent learners for life.

With better organization, better focus and time management, their next academic year could help them gain the confidence they need to stand out from the crowd.

Creating a Personal Brand

Standing out from the crowd means you have to work on the way others perceive you. In today's tech-centered world, our public personas are often created by our social media posts. Students must learn to develop their own 'personal brand'. This means that they must always be working on being the best version of themselves and portraying that to the outside world.

> *Never post to social media something you wouldn't say or do in front of a large audience.* — *Anonymous*

Our children aren't always the most forward-thinking and they may post things that are meant for friends but are inappropriate. When these posts are seen by teachers, by other students or by parents, they can negatively affect people's perceptions of your child.

Teenagers who are irresponsible with posts can even find that their bad judgment dogs their college applications and job interviews. The Internet is an unforgiving medium and items we post can last forever, even when we delete them, if they are picked up by fellow users.

As parents, we have to manage the social media accounts of our children to ensure that they are not posting items that may negatively affect their futures and make them stand out from the crowd for all the wrong reasons.

The best way to ensure that your child is portraying themselves appropriately on social media is to ask them to stop for just a second before they post and ask themselves these questions:

1. Is it kind?

2. Is it respectful?

3. Is it positive?

4. Does this reflect who I am and what I want to be?

> *Did You Know?*
>
> *If you plan a career in law enforcement think carefully about your profile on social media. "Social media and the digital footprint it leaves also complicates life for intelligence officers working undercover, especially younger officers who are part of the social media generation and who have not been very careful with what they post."[79] — STRATFOR*

Asking your child to think about who and what they want to be is a wonderful way to set life goals. It also helps them to regulate their own behavior. If they know where they are headed as a person, they are more likely to question behavior that doesn't fit into the concept of who they are.

Ideals to aspire to can include being kind, being determined, being successful, volunteering, making the world a better place, being a winner, and putting family first. When they have a cohesive idea of who they are, they will be confident and that is the surest way for them to stand out.

Everyone has the need to vent; negative feelings need to be expressed and we all understand that. But social media isn't the best place for airing grievances.

Your child's personal brand is also made up by their appearance, behavior, and the way they communicate. While individual style should be encouraged, they should also understand that people do judge a book by its cover.

Focus on Communication

Good communication skills are pivotal in learning and in life. If your child is able to communicate their ideas effectively, they will really stand out from the crowd. Imagine if your child is super smart, but their reading and writing skills aren't at the same level. They will have the smarts to do well at school, but will not be able to communicate their thoughts effectively on assignments and in exams.

Encourage reading at every age to help your child to be an effective communicator. Reading helps expand minds and vocabularies and helps build sentence structures.

Work on confidence building and encourage them to express their ideas. If they are shy, urge them to push their boundaries, role play different scenarios so that they feel more confident and reward their efforts with praise.

Enabling your child to stand out from the crowd means being proactive about his or her future. Set goals, work on confidence, and create considerate students who are a wonderful addition to any class.

5.2 The Well-Rounded Student: What Colleges are Looking for Today

By Steve Magat

Steve Magat has a personal passion for youth activities and educational programs including sports and Scouting. He especially believes in the personal value of innovation through action. Steve continues to make a difference in the lives of children within his community by coaching youth soccer and basketball teams in Henrico County, as well as a referee for GRAL and YMCA swimming. Steve serves as Committee Chair for Boy Scout Troop 776 and also serves on the School

Committee for Temple Beth-El of Richmond, VA and on the Board for BBYO Eastern Region. Steve is a devoted husband and a father of two active school-age boys. When Steve isn't working, he's either gardening, trying to play golf or rooting for his beloved NY Football Giants.

THE SEVEN THINGS THAT COLLEGES ARE LOOKING FOR TODAY

So you want to go to college. Your parents want you to go to XYZ University, but you want to go to ZYX College and your last report card says that you're not going to go anywhere until you get your Geometry grade up. So, how do you get into the college of your choice? How do you decide where to go? More importantly, with 3.45 million (approximately) applications filed each year, how do colleges decide who gets in?

College can be a $100,000 investment and to some parents and students, getting into the "right" school is the most important thing. Some parents think that acceptance into certain schools is an entitlement and are disappointed and surprised when reality hits. One of my clients lamented to me that her daughter was a solid 'B' student and was furious that her guidance counselor said that there was "no way" that she could get into the University of Virginia.

On the other end of the spectrum, I was working at a college fair at our local high school. The place was packed with parents and Junior and Senior students wading through tables filled with literature and lanyards, when all of a sudden I see one of my students, a seventh grader, and his father. His father wanted his son to start prepping for college! In middle school!

The father was from India and wasn't familiar with the concept of getting into college in America. He insisted that as long as his son was in the "Gifted Program" and the "International Baccalaureate" program then his son would certainly make it into Harvard! It was very eye opening to him when I introduced the concept of "the seven things that colleges are looking for today".

Colleges are competitive and seats/dorm rooms are limited. Acceptance rates at the most exclusive schools can hover in the 5–10 percent range while other top rated universities still accept fewer than 35 percent of the applicants. For example, here are some statistics for the class of 2018 directly from some of the more competitive schools in the U.S.:

University	Number of Applications	Number of Offers	Acceptance Rate (%)
Stanford	42,167	2,138	5
Yale	30,932	1,935	6
Vanderbilt	29,490	3634	12
Notre Dame	17,897	3,720	21
University of Virginia	31,042	8,970	29

College	Number of Applications	Number of Offers	Acceptance Rate (%)
Davidson	5,558	1,169	21
College of William & Mary	14,545	4,738	33
Virginia Tech	20,897	14,230	68

Imagine for a minute that you're on the other side of the application table. You work for a major university and you have 31,000 applications in front of you. You have 9,000 spaces to fill and you have to tell 22,000 very smart students whom you've never met before, that they're not good enough to attend your school. Which 22,000 students get the boot? What are you as an admissions representative looking for in a student? How do you figure out who stays and who just doesn't fit the criteria, the direction, and the history of your institution? How are you going to make your university a better place? Sometimes it's not fair, but who said life was fair.

All schools have specific criteria for their student body. Take a look at any university website and you will see the Freshman Profile of their most recent class and you can get an idea of what the average student is.

You can learn a lot from a school's website, and I always recommend that before you go out and buy a sweatshirt and brag to your friends that you're going to XYZ, you do a Google search first. You'll find information such as, how many students were in the top 10 or 20 percent of their graduating class? How many students were their class Valedictorians and Salutatorians? What's the ratio of men to women? Average SAT or ACT Score? Do you need to take an entrance exam? Average GPA? What's the percentage minority and international students, etc.?

Look at the site for clues then compare these clues to where you currently stand and be honest with yourself. You may need an impartial third party to help you out with this task. You "ain't" getting into Yale with a 1400 SAT score and a 3.8 GPA. Maybe you're setting your sights too low if you have a 4.6 GPA and you're in the top 10 percent of your class.

If websites confuse you or if you're not happy with the search results, the next task is to pay your guidance counselor a visit. You remember your guidance counselor right? This would be the person you were introduced to on the first day of ninth grade and haven't seen since. These people make it their job to give you clues as to what school may be the right fit for you. And you know what? They're very good at what they do, and generally, want to know you better and want to see you succeed. Remember, there's no such thing as the "Best School". You're looking for the "Best School for you" and your counselor can get you on your way. Best of all, they're not your parents!

When you talk to your counselor, he or she will tell you how to tip the odds of getting into your chosen school in your favor. They will help you set goals and send you in the right direction.

Most universities are looking for well-rounded students who will make their campuses better places. What could be worse than a campus of students who did nothing but spend hours upon hours at the library mastering calculus? Colleges want the brightest students who will make classes lively, fill up their football stadium, make active sororities and fraternities who give back to the community and make their daily newspapers thrive.

There are also ways to get into your college of choice even if you got a 'C' in Calculus and your English teacher "didn't like you". Universities all have their own standards. However, there are seven basic admission criteria that every school follows. Addressing these in your high school years will make the application madness more bearable.

Along with these criteria are ways that you can stand out in that 31,000 piece application pile. Some of these may elicit the response "Thanks captain obvious" while others might scream, "Oh my god! I never thought of that!" Regardless of how you feel about this list, the three most important words for you will be Relax ... relax ... relax. And the three most important things that you should remember are:

- Do your research

- Keep your grades up, and

- Enjoy high school!

1. GRADES AND UPWARD TREND

Grades are always the bottom line, and it seems so obvious. If you do well in school, you'll get to go to the college of your choice. Many students get discouraged, however, when they have a bad freshman year or if they get a 'C' in Algebra II. Fear not, though. Yes, it's true that sometimes you need to get straight As, but sometimes you as a student can offer something more to a campus than grades. A college may overlook one bad grade if they see an outstanding sophomore or junior year. The key is an upward trend. A 'B' in the first semester that became an 'A' in the second semester shows potential schools that the student has turned a corner academically, and has learned from their errors. If those grades aren't where they're supposed to be, get help. A tutor will build your confidence, study skills, and grades. Confidence is everything, along with hard work. When you're studying or doing homework, remember the 10-minute rule. Many school systems use the criteria of 10 minutes of actual homework per grade per night. If you're in ninth grade and you're not doing 90 minutes of homework, you can work a little harder. If it's taking you three hours to get your work done, maybe you're not using your time as effectively as you should. Build your study skills by working with a professional tutor or at least with a study buddy. If you've gotten through middle school by doing your homework on the living room couch with SpongeBob playing in the background and your smartphone on your lap, you probably need to work on those skills. High school academics can be hard! You're not a kid anymore.

Surprise ... if you do your homework well, chances are your grades will go up. If that's not working, remember the 'C' word—Confidence. Have the confidence to tell your teacher that you need some help. Don't be shy. Teachers love to be asked for help.

2. CLASS RIGOR

Take the toughest classes your school offers. Be it AP's (Advanced Placement), IB's (International Baccalaureate), or college level, take the toughest classes you can find. Don't be afraid! I remember several years back when my wife and I were invited to the AP fair at my son's high school. I really thought there would be a few dozen sets of parents and a couple of school administrators at the event. Much to my surprise, we arrived to a standing room only auditorium and hallways filled with nervous parents who remember what AP classes were like back in the 70s and 80s.

One of the highlights of the presentation was a panel of current seniors talking of their AP experiences. Of the six students who were speaking, four of them took at least three AP's in their junior year and one student actually took five AP classes and spoke of it like it was no big deal! The lesson here is that if you sign up for a class, approach it like you would any other class. You're SMART! You're confident! Your teacher will help you not only pass the class but succeed on the exam.

Oh by the way, if you're taking AP or IB classes, you will have better, more qualified teachers who really want to see you succeed. If you ask, they will help you become a better student and what better way to learn than to have someone who really believes in you?

If you don't know what the hardest classes are, ask a senior, or ask your guidance counselor. They know, and they'll also steer you in the right direction. There can be more than one "toughest class." Your friends and counselors also know the teachers and may be able to tell you what teacher may be a better fit for you. Colleges will tell you that AP and IB grades don't necessarily guarantee admission into their schools. I was at a seminar last fall with several Ivy League schools and one of the parents asked a question about their "Gifted" child in the IB program and that they have an advantage over a student in a "neighborhood" school. You should have heard the commotion when one by one, the college reps confirmed that IB didn't necessarily guarantee admission to their institutions!

3. QUALITY INVOLVEMENT IN EXTRACURRICULAR ACTIVITIES BOTH IN AND OUT OF SCHOOL

To some families, study, study, study, without regard for activities outside of school is the rule. If there's not a grade attached to it, it's not important. And by extracurricular activities, we're not just talking teams though it won't hurt to be on a team. OK, so you're not an athlete. Become one! You don't have to be an athlete to be on a sports team. There are sports which are also life skills. Life skills are just as important as book skills. Physical activity is a cornerstone to a healthy lifestyle so why not start the habit in high school? It drives me crazy when I ask high school students what they do after school and I hear "not much." One of the first things I say to these students is, "OK, tomorrow you're on the track team." Tryouts for some sports including track usually aren't necessary as meets are usually, "the more the merrier." Maybe track is taken a bit more seriously in your part of the country but any other individual sport— swimming, tennis, boxing, martial arts, and golf, for example— are great for a couple of reasons:

- Usually you don't need to try out

- There are other people on the team who have little or no experience

- They're great social opportunities—boys and girls sometimes practice or at least hang out together

I also ask students, what foreign language they take. My answer to that is, "Great! Tomorrow you're in the Spanish/French/Latin club. Language clubs usually end the year or have a Spring Break trip to some exotic locale. And next year, run for president of the club but not vice president. They do all the work." School activities are for EVERYONE. If you like something, do it. If you like something and there's not a club for it, start one in your school. If you and your friends play role playing games, make it an official club in your school! Not only would you have participated, you will have shown initiative in forming one. If it's a bust, maybe after you've moved on, new students will complete your legacy. How cool is that?

Youth groups like Young Life, BBYO, Scouting, and Boys & Girls Clubs are tremendous outlets for extracurricular activities. These national organizations, plus many others are widely recognized by admissions counselors and fulfill the need of adding activity to the college community. They also will lead to the topic we cover in the next section.

4. STRONG RECORD OF COMMUNITY SERVICE

It amazes me that I'll talk to some students who have scores and scores of community service hours and other students who barely have any. Service is a hallmark of great communities. Still, many students tell me that there aren't any opportunities around to perform community service. There are plenty of opportunities but sometimes it takes a little prodding and even some participation from Mom and Dad. Teach your parents that community service is important, and they might enjoy it too.

You like animals? Animal rescue groups need people to walk dogs at adoption sights. (My gym has a "Jog A Dog" program every Saturday for animal rescue.)

Sports fan? Little league needs umpires, grass cutters, and concession workers. In my town, there's usually a 5K race somewhere that needs volunteers.

Musician? Play piano for a senior home or YMCA and you're golden!

Organizations love teens! You're fun, you're exciting, you're attractive. Your enthusiasm brings in other enthusiastic people. Volunteering doesn't mean it has to be boring and if you're lucky, you might even get lunch and a free T-Shirt.

Boy and Girl Scouts—fantastic organizations that participate in food drives, environmental clean-ups, and other community events. One year in Scouts can easily mean fifty hours of community service while also doing something that may actually be fun with other kids your age. They also offer opportunities to lead. Earn Eagle Scout or Gold Award and you automatically get a plus mark in your favor. Yes, it's a data point along the way. Yes, there were just under 52,000 Eagle Scout awards conferred in the U.S. in 2014 but in my home state of Virginia, College of William and Mary, James Madison University, University of Virginia, and Virginia Tech combined alone received about 90,000 applications—51,820 people nationwide seems like a very small exclusive number.

5. RECOMMENDATIONS FROM TEACHERS AND COMMUNITY LEADERS

You say you're great. Your parents say you're great. Your uncle Phil says you're great but how great would it be if your principal who got his doctorate from your university of choice says you're great? What about your AP Calculus teacher who just happens to be on the scholarship committee for your safety school?

Bottom line, you need recommendations either from teachers or from members of the community. You won't need dozens, but six or seven nice letters that say how wonderful you are will take care of your top choices. Guess what? Your teachers are people too. They may also only be in their late twenties. When you graduate, they may be co-workers, neighbors, or dare I say, friends! It's never too early to begin networking. Your neighbor who you've been babysitting for over the last three years may just work in the HR department for a major employer in the area. Remember earlier when I told you to ask for help if you're not getting the grades you want in a certain subject? Your teacher will remember how nicely you asked, and how well your grades improved after you talked together. That makes you memorable and your teacher will love writing you a recommendation.

6. TEST SCORES

Yes, colleges look at test scores. That's just a fact. Why? According to the College Board, it's important for several reasons:

- It tests what you already know. It gives both you and colleges a sense of how you'll be able to apply the thinking, writing, and study skills required for college coursework.

- It's fair. The test is straightforward. There are no tricks designed to trip you up. Students who do well in the classroom are often the same ones who will do well on the SAT.

- It's more than just a test. The SAT also provides the opportunity for you to connect to scholarship opportunities, place out of certain college courses, and learn more about your academic strengths. (My primary reason for telling students to take these tests.) We always hear that teachers don't teach, "They only teach to the test." Well, in real life, you'll have tests. Some just count more than others.

According to the Educational Testing Service, the ACT is based on information your student is learning in high school.

Taking the test:

- Lets your student know if they are on track for college

- Points out a student's academic strengths and areas for improvement

- Identifies how your student can prepare to succeed in college or a career

- Enables a student to develop personalized career information

- Develops a comprehensive profile that tells colleges about your student's work in high school and their plans for the future

- Allows your student to connect with colleges and scholarship agencies that may be interested in him or her.

The bottom line here is that the tests are just one of the seven factors that schools take into consideration when making their decision. They are important only to the extent that you think they're important. Don't take them lightly as you will no doubt have other tests in your career.

Schools that don't require taking the SAT or ACT include:

- Christopher Newport

- Brandeis

- Wake Forest

- Temple

- Virginia Commonwealth University

And there are others throughout the country. Just because your school doesn't require an entrance exam, it doesn't mean that there aren't other factors involved in selection. The five previous factors are always in play and you may need to be a little more creative with the dreaded essay.

If you are applying to colleges that do not require an admissions exam or have test flexible options, it will help you to reflect on your strengths and weaknesses. Will the scores strengthen your overall application, or do they not truly represent your skills and abilities? Where do you shine the brightest?

While test optional policies give you yet another thing to think about as you apply, ultimately having that increased choice can only work in your benefit. By making an informed and intentional decision, you have the power to shape the story you tell to admissions officers.

7. PERSONAL STATEMENT

College essays are important because they let you reveal your personality. They can give admission officers a sense of who you are, as well as a chance to showcase your writing skills. Writing is hard but you've been doing it since first grade when you had to put together your first, "What I did on my summer vacation" poster.

First, it was fun. Then you had to learn what a noun was. Then a verb. Then you had to learn how to be specific. Then you had to write a book report and before you knew it, you were a writer! But, do you know how to write about yourself? Do you know about what's happening in the world today? Do you know how to talk about interesting things that have happened to you? Of course, you do! Now you have to write with a purpose. You have to make that purpose interesting.

Let's go back to the beginning of the chapter and pretend that you're an admissions officer with 31,000 applications in front of you. You and your colleagues have already eliminated 15,000 students because of grades and lack of class standing and test scores so now you've got 16,000 pieces of paper which need to be whittled down to 8,000. Hmmm, 16,000 500-word essays: that's eight million words answering the question, "Why should we accept you into our university?" That's 16,000 stories about how your parents overcame obstacles to immigrate to the U.S. and how you had to teach your parents English. It's 16,000 stories about how you would wake up at 5:30 a.m. to practice the trombone; go to school all day; then work at Pizza Hut in the evening and 16,000 stories about how your mission trip to Honduras changed your perspective on your comfortable middle-class life. But maybe your life isn't that ... er ... interesting. Maybe you're just you and you want to go to the best school. Or the school with the best football team, or the school with the best food. Now I have to write an essay! Starting the essay can be the hardest part. One of the best ways to start is by first creating a resume for yourself.

A resume is a list of "stuff" you've done over your career. I'm sure you've done more than just take selfies and play video games. Your resume is a summary of you. Did you win any awards? Did you succeed in something? Were you on a team? You don't have to do this by yourself. Your parents, other relatives, religious mentors, coaches, teachers, friends — hopefully, you have many people in your network who know what you've done. If you like what you see, great! If not, maybe it's time to do more "stuff". Remember, it's never too late to make the first step. Colleges are looking for "Upward Trends".

Secondly, I like to do what's called a brain dump. A brain dump is brainstorming about your personality traits and your strengths. Make a list of adjectives that describe yourself. Don't do it on a computer. Write it down. Write each trait in big letters. Lines on the page? Who needs lines on the page? Bring out your creative side.

Then take it a step further. Look at those traits and develop a statement. That sentence may bring out different things that you like or don't like about yourself. Maybe you remember an embarrassing moment that may seem silly, but with a little finesse, can become a very interesting story that will catch the readers' eye. The more unique the better! One of the favorite essays that I've seen was a story my son (OK, I like to brag about my kids) wrote about how in fourth grade, his Velcro warm-up pants came off in the middle of a relay race. It was a minor incident but it stuck with him all these years and he was able to craft it into an essay that got him into his choice of schools. His English teacher liked it so much that she asked if she could show it to her future classes as an example of what can be done with a college essay to stand out. Don't be afraid to show your work to a parent or to a teacher!

So what should my essay look like? Develop three essay parts:

Introduction: One paragraph that introduces your essay.

Body: Several paragraphs explaining the main idea with examples.

Conclusion: One paragraph that summarizes and ends the essay.

In academia this is known as "Tell me what you're going to write about," then "Tell it in more detail" and then "Summarize what you've just written about." If you master this, you will master the approach to writing most essays at the post-secondary level. It's never too early to start!

Remember, that essay is usually sent in an electronic application and 500 words means 500 words. Anything over 500 words won't fit in the little box so pay attention to your word count and make sure that your thoughts don't get cut off mid-sentence. Weak grammar and/or spelling at the beginning or end of an essay will automatically put yours in the reject pile.

Conclusion

College can be a $100,000 investment and it's NOT an entitlement. The key for students and parents to remember is that it's not just test scores and an 'A' in Algebra II. Colleges are competitive and you want to stand out among the competition. I was talking to a friend of mine who is an admissions representative at a large university and sometimes they have to say, "We have enough boys with 4.2 GPAs who played soccer and were in the Spanish Club." It sounds weird and not fair but life is sometimes weird and not fair. If a university has dorms and classrooms for 9,000 freshmen, and 31,000 applications come in, then 22,000 smart students are going to have to move on to school choice #2. Even if you use the 80/20 rule that of the 31,000 applicants, less than 25,000 applicants would qualify for the freshman class, and only one-third of the qualified applicants can actually attend, there needs to be something that you can quickly tell an overworked perfect stranger that you're worthy of attending their school.

Your family probably didn't donate a wing to the Chemistry building and your uncle probably didn't win the Heisman trophy so you as a great student must do everything in your power to get into your choice of schools but when you boil everything down, it comes down to seven things that will increase your odds of getting into your choice. Seven things that schools are looking for today. We might even boil those seven things down to three:

- Keep those grades up

- Work hard

- Do STUFF.

Good luck to everyone and enjoy your high school years.

Endnotes

1. Dweck, C., Walton, G., & Cohen, G. (2014*). Academic Tenacity: Mindsets and Skills that Promote Long-Term Learning.* Bill & Melinda Gates Foundation.

2. Parvizi et al.. (2013). Numerical processing in the human parietal cortex during experimental and natural conditions. *Nature Communications*, 4(2528).

3. Hanson, R. (2009). *Meditations to Change Your Brain—Rewire your Neural Pathways to Transform Your Life.* Published by Sounds True.

4. Shatz, C. (1992). The developing brain. *Scientific American*, 267(3), 60-67.

5. Clark, B. et al. (2014). The power of the mind: the cortex as a critical determinant of muscle strength/weakness. *Journal of Neurophysiology*, 112(12, 3219-3226).

6. Covey, S. R. (2004). *The 7 habits of highly effective people: Restoring the character ethic* .New York: Free Press.

7. Freedman, L. (2013). *The Developmental Disconnect in Choosing a Major: Why Institutions Should Prohibit Choice until Second Year.* Retrieved 21 September 2016, from https://dus.psu.edu/mentor/2013/06/disconnect-choosing-major/

8. Patel, N. (24 June 2014). The Psychology of Instant Gratification and How It Will Revolutionize Your Marketing Approach. [Weblog]. Retrieved 27 May 2016, from https://www.entrepreneur.com/article/235088

9. Byrne, R. (2006). *The Secret.* New York: Atria Books.

10. Clarey, C. (2014). Olympians Use Imagery as Mental Training. *The New York Times*, February 22, 2014. Retrieved 6 June, 2016, from http://www.nytimes.com/2014/02/23/sports/olympics/olympians-use-imagery-as-mental-training.html?_r=0

11. McCormack, M. (1984). *What They Don't Teach You at Harvard Business School.* New York: Bantam Books.

12. Schippers, M.C, Scheepers, A & Peterson, J.P. (2015). A scalable goal-setting intervention closes both the gender and ethnic minority achievement gap. *Palgrave Communications*, 1(15014).

13. Latham, G. P. and Locke, E. A. (1991). Self-regulation through goal setting. *Organizational Behavior and Human Decision Processes*; 50 (2): 212–247.

14. Oettingen, G, Pak H-j and Schnetter, K. (2001). Self-regulation of goal-setting: Turning free fantasies about the future into binding goals. *Journal of Personality and Social Psychology*; 80 (5): 736–753.

15. Grant, A. M., Franklin, J. and Langford, P. (2002). The self-reflection and insight scale: A new measure of private self-consciousness. *Social behavior and Personality*; 30 (8): 821–836.

16. Bandura, A. (1997). *Self-efficacy: The exercise of control.* New York: Freeman.

17. Locke, E. A. and Latham, G. P. (1990) *A Theory of Goal-Setting and Task Performance.* Prentice Hall: Englewood Cliffs, NJ.

18. Covey, S. (1989). *The 7 Habits of Highly Effective People: Powerful Lessons in Personal Change.* New York: Free Press.

19. Locke and Latham. *A Theory of Goal-Setting and Task Performance.*

20. Ibid.

21. Schunk, D. H. (1995). Self-efficacy and education and instruction. In J. E. Maddux (Ed.), *Self-efficacy, adaptation, and adjustment: Theory, research, and application* (p. 281–303). New York: Plenum Press.

22. Ibid.

23. Locke, E. A. and Latham, G. P. (1990) *A Theory of Goal-Setting and Task Performance.* Prentice Hall: Englewood Cliffs, NJ.

24. Covey, S. (1989). *The 7 Habits of Highly Effective People: Powerful Lessons in Personal Change.* New York: Free Press.

25. Maslow, A. H. (1943). A theory of human motivation. *Psychological review*, 50(4), 370.

26. Herzberg, F., (1973). *Work and the Nature of Man.* New York: Mentor Book, The New America Library, Inc.

27. Bandura, A., (1986). The Explanatory and Predictive Scope of Self-Efficacy Theory. *Journal of Social and Clinical Psychology*: Vol. 4, Special Issue: Self-Efficacy Theory in Contemporary Psychology (p. 359–373).

28. Bandura, A. (1992). Social cognitive theory and social referencing. In S. Feinman (Ed.), *Social Referencing and the Social Construction of Reality in Infancy* (p. 175–208). New York: Plenum Press.

29. Bandura, A. (1992a). Exercise of personal agency through the self-efficacy mechanism. In R. Schwarzer (Ed.), *Self-efficacy: Thought control of action* (p. 3–38). Washington: Hemisphere.

30. Bandura, A., and Schunk, D. H. (1981). Cultivating competence, self-efficacy, and intrinsic interest through proximal self-motivation. *Journal of Personality and Social Psychology*, 41, 586–598.

31. Bandura, A., Barbaranelli, C., Caprara, G. V., and Pastorelli, C. (1996). Multifaceted impact of self-efficacy beliefs on academic functioning. *Child Development*, 67, 1206–1222.

32. Crossman, A. (2011). *Study Smart, Study Less*. New York: Ten Speed Press.

33. Ibid. p. 90.

34. Slocum, D. (2005). Leading the Future of Learning through Four Key Trends. *Forbes Magazine*, February 17.

35. Brown, J. and Duguid, P. (1995). "Stolen Knowledge" *Educational Technology*. 33(3), 10–15.

36. Noam, E. M., (1995). Electronics and the Dim Future of the University, *Science*, 270(5234), p.247–249.

37. Fischer, G. & Scharff, E., (1998). Learning Technologies in Support of Self-Directed Learning. Journal of Interactive Media in Education. 1998(2), p.Art. 4.

38. Aspin, D and Chapman, J. (2006). Lifelong Learning: Concepts and Conceptions. *International Journal of Lifelong Education*, 19(1), 19–38.

39. Dawson, P. and Guare, R. (2009). *Smart But Scattered: The Revolutionary "Executive Skills" Approach to Helping Kids Reach Their Potential*. New York: The Guilford Press.

40. Ibid.

41. Dauncey, M. (2014). "Nutrition, the brain and cognitive decline: insights from epigenetics." *European Journal of Clinical Nutrition*, 68(11):1179–85.

42. Colbin, A. (1986). *Food and Healing: How what you eat determines your health, your well-being, and the quality of your life.* Toronto: Random House, p. 36.

43. Ervin, R.B, Kit, B., Margaret D. Carroll, M.D., Ogden, C.L. (2012). "Consumption of Added Sugar among U.S. Children and Adolescents 2005–2008." *NCHS Data Brief*, no. 87. Hyattsville, MD: National Center for Health Statistics.

44. *Sources of Added Sugar in the Diets of the U.S. Population Ages 2 Year and Older,* Retrieved 10 October 2016, from http://www.timigustafson.com/2010/way-too-sweet/

45. Nyaradi, A., Foster, J.K., Hickling, S., Li, J., Ambrosini, G.L., Jacques, A., Oddy, W.H. (2014). "Prospective associations between dietary patterns and cognitive performance during adolescence." *Journal of Child Psychology and Psychiatry*, 55(9).

46. Nyaradi, A., Li, J., Hickling, S., Foster, J.K., Jacques, A., Ambrosini, G.L., Oddy, W.H. 2015. "A western dietary pattern is associated with poor academic performance in Australian adolescents." *Nutrients*, 7(4): 2961-2982. Published online 2015 Apr 17. doi: 10.3390/nu7042961.

47. Lustig, R. (2009). *Sugar: The Bitter Truth.* UCSF Osher Center for Integrative Medicine. UCTV.

48. Sanchez, A., Reeser, J.L., Lau, H.S., Yahiku, P.Y., Willard, R.E., McMillan, P.J., Cho, S.Y., Magie, A.R., Register, U.D. 1973. "Role of sugars in human neutrophilic phagocytosis." *The American Journal of Clinical Nutrition,* 26: 1180–1184.

49. Haas, E. (2006). *Staying Healthy with Nutrition: The Complete Guide to Diet and Nutritional Medicine.* Berkeley: Celestial Arts.

50. Ibid.

51. Nieh, E, Matthews, G et al. (2015). "Decoding Neural Circuits that Control Compulsive Sucrose Seeking." Cell, vol.160, no.3, 528–541.

52. Blumenthal, D and Gold, M. (2010). Neurobiology of Food Addiction, *Clinical Nutrition and Metabolic Care,* 13:359–365.

53. Basciano, H., Federico, L., Adeli, K. (2005). Fructose, insulin resistance and metabolic dyslipidemia. *Nutrition and Metabolism,* 2(5). doi:10.1186/1743-7075-2-5. Lustig, 2009.

54. Mercola, J. (2013). Confirmed—Fructose Can Increase Your Hunger and Lead to Overeating. Retrieved 21 September 2016, from http://articles.mercola.com/sites/articles/archive/2013/01/14/fructose-spurs-overeating.aspx. Viewed September 21, 2016.

55. Ibid.

56. Suez, J., Korem, T., Zeevi, D., Zilberman-Schapira, et al. (2014). Artificial sweeteners induce glucose intolerance by altering the gut microbiota. *Nature,* 514:181–186. doi:10.1038/nature13793

57. Ashok, I. and Sheeladevi, R. (2014). Biochemical responses and mitochondrial mediated activation of apoptosis on long-term effect of aspartame in rat brain. *Redox Biology,* 2:820-831. doi:10,1016/j.redox.2014.04.011

58. Steinberg, L. (2011). *You and Your Adolescent: The Essential Guide for Ages 10–25.* New York, NY: Simon and Shuster.

59. Benton, D., Winichagoon, P., Tze P., Ng, Tee, E., Isabelle, M. (2012). Symposium on nutrition and cognition: towards research and application for different life stages. *Asia Pacific Journal of Clinical Nutrition,* 21(1):104-124.

60. Bainbridge, David (2008). *Beyond the Zonules of Zinn: A Fantastic Journey Through Your Brain.* United States of America: Harvard University Press, 31.

61. Benton, 2012.

62. Smith, M., Scholey, A. (2014). Nutritional influences on human neurocognitive functioning. *Frontiers in Human Neuroscience,* 8(358). Published online 2014 May 27. doi: 10.3389/fnhum.2014.00358.

63. Herbert, T.B., Cohen, S. (1993). "Stress and immunity in humans: a meta-analytic review." *Psychosomatic Medicine,* 55(4): 364-79.

64. Lupien, S.J., Maheu, F., Tu, M., Fiocco, A., Schramek, T.E. (2007). The effects of stress and stress hormones on human cognition: Implications for the field of brain and cognition. *Brain and Cognition,* 65(3): 209–237.

65. Conrad, C. (2008). Chronic Stress-Induced Hippocampal Vulnerability: the Glucocorticoid Vulnerability Hypothesis. *Rev Neuroscience,* 19(6): 395–411.

66. Glaser, R., Stress-induced immune dysfunction: implications for health, *Nature Reviews Immunology*, 5: 243–251.

67. Conrad, C. (2008). 19(6): 395–411.

68. Dusek, J., Out, H., Wohlhuerter, A.L. et al. (2008). Genomic Counter-Stress Changes Induced by the Relaxation Response. *PLOS One*, 3(7): e2576. DOI: 10.1371/journal.pone.0002576.

69. Demers, C. (2013). How to Change Your Stress Response. *Yoga International*. www.yogainternational.com. Accessed September 21, 2016.

70. Ratey, J. (2008). *Spark: The Revolutionary New Science of Exercise and the Brain*. New York: Little, Brown and Company.

71. Ibid, p. 19.

72. Yamada, K, Nabeshima, T. (2013). Brain-derived neurotrophic factor/TrkB signaling in memory processes. *Pharmacological Science*, 91(4): 267-70. doi:10.1254/jphs.91.267.

73. Cheatham, C. (2014). Mechanisms and correlates of a healthy brain: A commentary. *Monographs of the Society for Research in Child Development*, 79(4): 156.

74. Ibid, p. 153–65.

75. de Souza, R. et al. (2015). Intake of saturated and trans unsaturated fatty acids and risk of all cause mortality, cardiovascular disease, and type 2 diabetes: systematic review and meta-analysis of observational studies. *British Medical Journal*, 351:h3978. doi: http://dx.doi.org/10.1136/bmj.h3978.

76. Simopoulos, A. (2003). Importance of the Ratio of Omega-6/Omega-3 Essential Fatty Acids: Evolutionary Aspects. In Simopoulos, Artemis P.; Cleland, L.G. Omega-6/Omega-3 Essential Fatty Acid Ratio: The Scientific Evidence. *World Review of Nutrition and Dietetics*, 92:1–22. doi:10.1159/000073788.

77. Matthews, G. (2015). Presentation to Ninth Annual International Conference of the Psychology Research Unit of Athens Institute for Education and Research (ATINER). Retrieved 25 September 2016, from www.dominican.edu/dominicannews/study-highlights-strategies-for-achieving-goals

78. *Summer learning loss*. Retrieved 25 September 2016, from https://en.wikipedia.org/wiki/Summer_learning_loss

79. STRATFOR (2015). "The Risk to Undercover Operatives in the Digital Age." *Security Weekly*. Retrieved 25 September 2016, from www.stratfor.com/weekly/ risk-undercover-operatives-digital-age.

Printed in Canada